O Blessed Night

O Blessed Night

Recovering from Addiction, Codependency and Attachment
based on the insights of St. John of the Cross and
Pierre Teilhard de Chardin

Francis Kelly Nemeck, OMI and
Marie Theresa Coombs, Hermit

ALBA·HOUSE   NEW·YORK

SOCIETY OF ST. PAUL, 2187 VICTORY BLVD., STATEN ISLAND, NY 10314

Library of Congress Cataloging-in-Publication Data

Nemeck, Francis Kelly, 1936-
    O Blessed Night : theological underpinnings for recovery from
addiction, codependecy, and attachment, according to St. John of
the Cross and Pierre Teilhard de Chardin / Francis Kelly Nemeck and
Marie Theresa Coombs.
        p.   cm.
    Extensively revised from F.K. Nemeck's thesis (doctoral),
published 1975 under title: Teilhard de Chardin et Jean de la Croix.
    Includes bibliographical references.
    ISBN 0-8189-0587-5
    1. Suffering — Religious aspects — Catholic Church — 2. Co-
dependence (Psychology) — Religious aspects — Christianity.
3. Substance abuse — Religious aspects — Christianity. 4. Catholic
Church — Doctrines. 5. Spirituality — Catholic Church. 6. John of
the Cross, Saint, 1542-1591. 7. Teilhard de Chardin, Pierre.
I. Coombs, Marie Theresa. II. Nemeck, Francis Kelly, 1936-
Teilhard de Chardin et Jean de la Croix. III. Title.
    BT732.7.N45   1991
    248.2 — dc20   90-19635
                                                            CIP

Designed, printed and bound in the United States of
America by the Fathers and Brothers of the
Society of St. Paul, 2187 Victory Boulevard,
Staten Island, New York 10314, as part of their
communications apostolate.

Printing Information:

Current Printing - first digit   2 3 4 5 6 7 8 9 10 11 12

Year of Current Printing - first year shown
                        1993   1994   1995   1996   1997   1998

TABLE OF CONTENTS

St. John of the Cross On Detachment

PRINCIPAL ABBREVIATIONS

AE	Pierre Teilhard de Chardin, *Activation of Energy*, Harcourt, 1970.
Ascent	St. John of the Cross, *The Ascent of Mount Carmel* (references are to the Spanish edition).
Called by God	*Marie Theresa Coombs & Francis Kelly Nemeck, Called by God: A Theology of Vocation and Lifelong Commitment*, MS, 1990.
Canticle	St. John of the Cross, *The Spiritual Canticle*, 2nd redaction (references are to the Spanish edition).
CE	Pierre Teilhard de Chardin, *Christianity and Evolution*, Harcourt, 1971.
Contemplation	Francis Kelly Nemeck & Marie Theresa Coombs, *Contemplation*, Liturgical Press, 1982.
Cor.	*Pierre Teilhard de Chardin and Maurice Blondel: Correspondence*, Herder and Herder, 1967.
DM	Pierre Teilhard de Chardin, *The Divine Milieu*, Harper Torchbooks, 1960.
Flame	St. John of the Cross, *The Living Flame of Love*, 2nd redaction (references are to the Spanish edition).
FM	Pierre Teilhard de Chardin, *The Future of Man*, Harper Torchbooks, 1964.
HE	Pierre Teilhard de Chardin, *Human Energy*, Harcourt, 1971.

HM	Pierre Teilhard de Chardin, *The Heart of Matter*, Harcourt, 1978.
HU	Pierre Teilhard de Chardin, *Hymn of the Universe*, Harper and Row, 1965.
Journal	Pierre Teilhard de Chardin, *Personal Journals*: I-XXI, 1915-1955.
LT	Pierre Teilhard de Chardin, *Letters from a Traveller*, Harper and Row, 1962.
MM	Pierre Teilhard de Chardin, *The Making of a Mind*, Harper and Row, 1965.
Night	St. John of the Cross, *The Dark Night of the Soul* (references are to the Spanish edition).
SC	Pierre Teilhard de Chardin, *Science and Christ*, Harper and Row, 1968.
Spiritual Direction	Francis Kelly Nemeck & Marie Theresa Coombs, *The Way of Spiritual Direction*, Liturgical Press, 1985.
Spiritual Journey	Francis Kelly Nemeck & Marie Theresa Coombs, *The Spiritual Journey: Critical Thresholds and Stages of Adult Spiritual Genesis*, Liturgical Press, 1987.
TF	Pierre Teilhard de Chardin, *Towards the Future*, Harcourt, 1975.
Writings	Pierre Teilhard de Chardin, *Writings in Time of War*, Harper and Row, 1969.

GENERAL NOTES

1. All translations from Hebrew, Greek, Latin, French and Spanish sources are our own. We ordinarily adapt these texts to reflect contemporary inclusive language.

2. Following the Western mystical tradition, we use the word "soul" in this study as synonymous with "person," stressing, however, the innermost recesses of personhood. Thus, our usage of the term transcends the classical scholastic *córpus-ánima* (body-soul) distinction. The mystical usage reflects biblical notions: the Hebrew *nephésh* (breath, person, soul) and the New Testament *psyché* (life, self, soul).

3. We profoundly respect the need for inclusive language in theological discourse. Yet, contemporary English syntax poses many problems in this regard. To strike a balance between the two factors, we follow these guidelines:

A. When using pronouns to refer to the human person, we always use s/he, him/her, etc.

B. In relation to God, we retain the biblical terms "Father" and "Lord." With regard to those and other names for God which are grammatically masculine, we employ the corresponding masculine pronouns.

C. We readily acknowledge the feminine dimension of God and the legitimacy of speaking of God as "Mother." For this reason, we refer to "God" as "s/he" in the nominative case. Yet, to keep the text from becoming unduly cumbersome, we do not use "him/her" in relation to the grammatically masculine noun "God." In reality, s/he transcends both masculine and feminine.

4. There are two peculiarities in Teilhard de Chardin's literary style which we note:

A. He often capitalizes words which ordinarily would not be capitalized in either French or English. He does this for emphasis or to draw attention to the special meaning he gives them. We have retained this element of his style, since it is helpful in interpreting certain passages: for example, *le Monde*, the World.

B. Teilhard coins and even creates certain words and technical expressions. Generally, we paraphrase these into intelligible English (e.g., *par traversée*, by going-all-the-way-through). Sometimes we transliterate them (e.g., *le Christique*, the Christic). Once in awhile, we retain the French word itself (e.g., *Milieu*, Milieu).

5. The original research which underlies this book began in the late 1960's as a doctoral study in Christian spirituality by Francis Kelly Nemeck under the direction of Henri de Lubac, S.J. Those studies led to a dissertation entitled *Les "passivités" dans la mystique teilhardienne* (1973).

That thesis, in turn, was co-published by Les Editions Desclée (Paris) and by Les Editions Bellarmin (Montreal) as volume 20 of their series *Hier/Aujourd'hui* under the title *Teilhard de Chardin et Jean de la Croix* (1975).

Later, the author translated and readapted the book into English recasting its focus in the direction of *Receptivity* (1985).

Here, the work has been completely re-thought, re-presented and co-authored in relation to recovery from addiction, codependency and attachment.

INTRODUCTION

This book has been a long time in the making. Its writing goes back over twenty years. Moreover, the basic question which it addresses has persisted in each of us as long as we can remember.

Philosophers refer to that question as "the problem of evil." Skeptics might phrase it: "If God is truly caring, why is there so much pain in the world?" Virtually everybody at one time or another has cried at least in his/her heart: "Why, Lord? Why must I suffer?" Even the mother of Jesus lamented: "Son, why have you done this to us?" (Lk 2:48).

This book addresses the issue of human pain, hurt and suffering.

That question can, however, be broached from many perspectives. Our point of view is the positive and constructive value inherent in human suffering as it relates to recovery from addiction, codependency and attachments. Thus, we focus on passing through pain to interior freedom as opposed to trying to avoid hurt at any cost.

We hope that our reflections are helpful to persons who are searching for a deeper faith understanding of the recovery process in which they are engaged. We also address our reflections to those whose faith is leading them to integrate into their self-understanding and ministry insights of contemporary psychology on recovery from addiction and codependency.

The instinct to avoid as much pain as possible is perfectly normal. All life — even animal and vegetative — naturally resists suffering. The crux of the question, therefore, is what

do we do with the pain that we cannot avoid? How do we cope
with inevitable suffering and ultimately with death?

The addictive, codependent and attached response is to
produce a quick fix for hurt or to devise a strategy for denying
its existence. Thus, addictions, codependency and attachments afford only the illusion of avoiding pain while in effect
causing more long-term suffering.

The response of the mature Christian is to face hurt
squarely and to pass through it in faith allowing God to recycle
the suffering into a salvific experience.

What do we mean by addiction, codependency and
attachment?

By *addiction* we understand any compulsive need to
revert habitually to a substance or ritual in order to alter one's
experience of reality. The addict resorts to that behavior
principally to flee the pain inherent in life. Every addiction
inflicts damage on the whole person. Depending on circumstances, however, that impairment can be more observable in
the physical, the mental, the emotional or the spiritual realms.
Addictions can range from substance abuse (e.g., heroin,
cocaine, caffeine, nicotine) to demanding that all people think
and act alike. Addiction, therefore, is a pathological relationship to a mood-altering experience that has life-damaging
consequences.

Codependency designates two principal patterns of interaction: (1) It denotes a style of relating wherein a person has
let someone else's behavior affect or control him/her and
becomes obsessed with controlling the other's actions. Thus,
codependency describes how I react to you as my primary
stressor. Over time, I create a way of being and behaving which
are dependent on your behavior or addiction. (2) Codependency refers also to a pattern of relating evident when an adult's
sense of identity is based on sources external to the self. Those
sources may be another person (e.g., a spouse, a parent), an
object (e.g., money, clothes, success, fun), a situation (e.g.,
work, gambling).

By *attachment* we mean any voluntary or spontaneous

arresting on a creature in such a manner as to diminish or to eliminate its providential role in our life. Even the slightest attachment impedes to some degree our spiritual journey — our transformation in God, our deification. Attachment therefore, is a disordered affect toward a person, situation or thing, which temporarily affords a happiness-fix. In so doing, it creates the illusion of assuaging pain, and it impedes spiritual growth. In this sense, addiction is the most extreme actualization of attachment.

Throughout this work, we understand "pain," "hurt," "suffering" equally from a subjective viewpoint and from an evolutionary perspective. Subjectively, they are both the anguish which we inflict on ourselves by our misguided actions and the misery which others heap upon us whether intentionally or accidentally. From an evolutionary perspective, suffering is the price that has to be paid for progress — that is, for moving through this world to God. In this mortal existence, nothing worthwhile comes easily.

God expects us to fight with him against evil. Divine providence urges us to minimize pain. If we have a headache, we take an aspirin. If we are in a bad mood, we seek out a friend to help us through it. We improve what we can. Yet, no one can indefinitely avoid suffering. Aspirins cannot cure all head problems. Friends cannot take away every sadness. There is no way to avoid all pain. Everyone dies sooner or later. We must learn to face pain peacefully and go through it joyfully. In that manner, suffering can have an enormously productive influence on our life:

> The cross looks like sheer foolishness to those
>   who are not on the way to salvation.
> But to those of us who are on the way,
>   we see it as God's power to save (1 Cor 1:18).

The cross is innately illogical to Christians and non-Christians alike. Yet, for true believers there is another perspective — faith. Faith enables us to encounter the Lord in suffering and beyond pain. So:

> While the Jews demand miracles
>   and the Greeks look for wisdom,
>   here we are preaching a crucified Christ:
> An insurmountable stumbling block to the Jews
>   and utter foolishness to the Gentiles,
>   but to those called by God — whether Jew or Greek —
>   a Christ who is the power and the wisdom of God.
> For God's foolishness is wiser than human wisdom, and
>   God's weakness is stronger than human strength
>
> (1 Cor 1:22-25).

In that vein, we entitle this book *O Blessed Night.* We use that phrase in the spirit of the *O Beata Nox!* of the Easter Vigil Proclamation and of the *noche dichosa* of St. John of the Cross. [1]

Paradox of all paradoxes! It is when we are weakest that we are strongest (2 Cor 12:10). Jesus was crucified out of weakness, yet he was raised up by the power of God. When he was most spent in his humanity, Christ's divinity definitively transformed that mortality into resurrection. In him, all human weakness is open to the same empowerment (2 Cor 13:4). Thus, the very pain which the addictive, codependent and attached personality tries so desperately to flee can become in God's providence a privileged instrument of deification (Rm 8:28-30). The happiness, peace and joy for which every human being irresistibly yearns (Ps 42:1-2; 63:1; 84:2) cannot be found in addiction, codependency or attachment to any creature, but only in letting go everything created and in loving abandonment to a Power-greater-than-oneself.

To guide our theological reflection on that mystery, we have chosen two spiritual masters: St. John of the Cross (1542-1591) and Pierre Teilhard de Chardin (1881-1955). Both drank passionately from the chalice of pain in their personal lives. Both experienced and pondered in their hearts the positive and constructive value of human suffering. Both wrote insightfully on the providential and transformative value inherent in working through hurt.

---

1. See stanzas 3-5 of the poem *En una noche oscura.*

John, for his part, accentuates the loving-purging dynamics intrinsic to breaking out of the attachment-addiction cycle. Teilhard, on the other hand, stresses from an evolutionary perspective the dynamics intrinsic to a healthy relationship with self, creation and God. Each author complements the other while imbibing deeply from the Gospel and Judeo-Christian mystical tradition.

There is an added incentive to discussing the theology of John of the Cross at this time. In 1991, we observe the four-hundredth anniversary of his death in Ubeda, Spain. He died at the age of forty-nine during the early morning hours of December 14th, after a long bout with osteomyelitis and gangrene. His spirituality remains perennially current.

There is also a special reason for discussing the theology of Teilhard in this context. In one of his earliest major essays — *The Mystical Milieu* (1917) — he affirms his conviction that every person is called to become an uncompromising realist:

> At the outset of his/her spiritual journey, the perception of God present in all things presupposed in the searcher an intense *zest* for *the Real*.
>
> A little later on, collaboration with God active in everything forced the pilgrim to develop as wide a *consciousness* as possible, again of *the Real*.
>
> Now that s/he is progressing further into the immanent God, the searcher is as committed as anyone to an unremitting *fulfillment*, always of *the Real*.
>
> That can mean only one thing: The passionate desire for union with God forces the sojourner *to give* created entities *their maximum degree of reality* — whether in his/her knowledge of and love for them or in their proper being.
>
> Thus, out of the depths of his/her vision — which some call a dream — the interiorly maturing pilgrim is *a supreme Realist.*[2]

Recovery from addiction, codependency and attachment

2. *Writings*, p. 139.

is a process of getting in touch with and accepting both our human reality as well as the Reality of a Power-greater-than-ourselves. Recovery is a major dynamic in our transformation in God who became incarnate and sends us forth:

> to proclaim freedom for those who are entrapped;
> to announce recovery for those who cannot see their way out;
> to herald release for those all tied up in knots (Lk 4:18);
> to signal liberation for those who not only fear death
>   (Heb 2:15), but also fear life.

ADDICTION, CODEPENDENCY AND ATTACHMENT

CHAPTER 1

ADDICTION, CODEPENDENCY AND ATTACHMENT

In the opening chapter of the Letter to the Colossians, we read:

> Christ is the image of the unseen God,
>   the firstborn of all creation.
> In him were created all things . . .
> Everything was created through him and for him . . .
> In him all things hold together (1:15-19).

That text epitomizes the fundamental relationship between God and creation. In Christ, divinity and humanity (together with the rest of creation) meet. In him, we are created and destined to transformation in God.

Because we are created in Christ, through him and for him, we cannot be satisfied until we reach the fullness of our destiny. In this mortal life, we remain sojourners. A relentless yearning in our spirit incites us to search further and to strain ever forward toward God:

> Our heart remains restless, O Lord,
>   until it rests in you. [1]

Our relationship with other persons and with creation is an essential dimension of our journey to the Father. Both

---

1. St. Augustine, *Confessions*, I, 1.

personal and nonpersonal creation have a providential role in
our quest for God. Provided that we relate to it correctly,
creation supports us, uplifts us, encourages us. Our involvement with it is meant to make us more lovingly receptive to the
Lord.

> Through the grandeur and beauty of creatures,
>   we can, by analogy, contemplate their Creator (Ws 13:5).

By our involvement with creation, we also contribute to its
becoming in Christ.

However, instead of letting creation open us to a Power-
greater-than-ourselves, we frequently try to make a particular
creature into a god. All too often we become engrossed with
creatures, trapped in our own disordered desires. Thus we
prevent creatures from fulfilling their providential role in our
regard.

History has seen the effects of many forms of disordered
desire. Three in particular have plagued human relationships
since "homo sapiens" first walked the face of the earth: addictions, codependency and attachments. Although these have
existed from the beginning, it is within recent times that we
have been able to name them more precisely and to offer
renewed hope for recovery from them.

A. *Addiction*

Addiction denotes a pathological relationship to a mood-
altering experience which has life-damaging consequences.

The word "relationship" in this context implies mutual-
ity; that is, connection between one person and another
person, object or event in such a way that each exerts influence
upon the other.

Most people, objects and situations have something to
contribute to our growth, provided we relate to them in a
healthy manner. For instance: A friend supports and

challenges us. A balanced diet enhances our physical well-being. During an illness, the proper drug restores us to health. Thus, a variety of sound relationships nurtures self-development.

Addiction, however, is a *pathological* relationship. It uses persons, objects or events for purposes that they cannot possibly fulfill. The addiction becomes the all-absorbing focus, the provider of ultimate meaning, the sole reason for being of the addict. Everything s/he does revolves increasingly around the object of desire. In that way, the addiction becomes a god to which the addict is completely subjected.

Addiction is also mood-altering. The intent of addicts is to eliminate pain and to secure pleasure. They use a fix to seek connectedness and intimacy. Whatever person or thing they find to serve that purpose is capable of becoming an addiction. The mood-alteration they experience in a stiff drink, a sniff of cocaine or a strong sleeping pill can become the hook that pulls them back repeatedly for more. The relief that they initially experience from immersing themselves in work or from relentlessly pursuing fun can keep alluring them until they are engrossed in it. The feeling of worth which results from helping others — whether they need it or not — can become a panacea for avoiding a sense of inferiority or low self-esteem.

Thus, the range of possible addictions extends beyond substances like alcohol, heroin, crack, cocaine, ice or marijuana. It embraces also compulsive use of milder chemicals such as caffeine, sugar or nicotine. Obsessions with a person (e.g., hero or movie star), with an activity (e.g., sex, work), with an object (e.g., food, guns), with an idea (e.g., dreaming of a romance) can all provide a fix. Moreover, qualities such as perfectionism, needing to be needed, success, specialness, knowledge, conformity, fun, control or relaxation can become addictive.

In addiction, the mood-altering experience produces life-damaging effects. The addict becomes emotionally, mentally and at times physically dependent upon the fix. S/he mistakes the excitement and the intensity of the experience for inti-

macy. The addict thus ceases fostering communion with self,
God and others in a quest for nurturance from the desired
object. The addict attempts to escape the pain of reality and to
create a fantasy world supposedly devoid of pain. In fleeing the
suffering inherent in the human journey, the addict loses zest
for life. Emotional numbness and loss of connectedness to
one's true self result.

The life-damaging consequence of addiction causes a
ripple effect on all aspects of life: health, relationships, work,
finances, leisure, spirituality, personality development, etc.
Addiction erodes every qualitative dimension of a person's
existence.

Addiction is present, therefore, whenever we rivet on
someone, something or some event in such a way that the
experience is simultaneously mood-altering, pain-avoiding
and life-damaging.

B. Codependency

The word "codependency" has different suppositions,
depending on the aspect of dependency one wishes to stress.

The term originated in reference to the spouse of an
alcoholic. Before long, its scope was broadened to include
attitudes toward life and patterns of behavior taken by a person
— whether spouse, child, friend or loved one — in order to
survive living with an addict. Thus a codependent person is
anyone who becomes fixed on constantly adapting to his/her
primary stressor.

Codependency in that sense is itself a form of addiction.
Maintaining control of the situation becomes a mood-altering,
pain-avoiding, life-damaging experience. The more the living
circumstances deteriorate, the harder codependent persons
work at keeping things together. In that way, they avoid facing
their inner pain as well as the unmanageability of life with an
addict. Codependency produces increasing alienation from
self and others.

Codependency can have an even broader meaning. It

refers also to a syndrome in which a person lets someone else's behavior affect and control him/her and becomes obsessed with controlling that other person's behavior.

A third way of understanding codependency is to view it as an immature manner of relating which occurs when an individual bases his/her identity almost exclusively on a source external to self. That source may be another person (e.g., a spouse, a parent), an object (e.g., money, clothes, success, fun) or a situation (e.g., work, betting).

Similar to the previous view is that of codependency as a psychological disorder caused by a person's failure to have completed the developmental task of establishing in early childhood a self separate and distinct from one's parents.

Understood as a pattern of behaviors and attitudes result-ing from a self-identity based on controlling another's behavior or on living by externals, codependency is possibly the addic-tion from which most other addictions arise.

Whatever the precise meaning one gives codependency, most people knowledgeable on the subject agree that code-pendent individuals exhibit the following characteristics and behavior patterns:

> Codependents mistake intensity and excitement for intimacy.
> They tend to choose friends, lovers, spouses who are addicted or themselves codependent.
> They are not attracted to marital partners and close friends who would be trustworthy and consistent in affection.
> They manifest a learned helplessness which leaves them blind to viable options and possible choices.
> They display a hopeless, no-way-out mentality.
> Control over all aspects of life is of utmost importance to them.
> They manipulate others in an effort to maintain control.
> They base their identity on sources outside themselves, for instance: a person, wealth, a career.
> They mistrust themselves and others.
> They lack clearly defined ego boundaries; i.e., they do not know their own needs, feelings and thoughts.

They caretake others to the point of self-neglect.

They feel bored and worthless if they don't have someone to help or a problem to solve.

They feel that they spend their whole life giving to others, with nobody giving to them in return.

They are frequently invasive and intrusive of others' boundaries.

They have difficulty communicating effectively.

They are often in a state of emotional numbness.

For many, shame is a state of being rather than a feeling.

They lack spontaneity.

They are hyper-vigilant and hyper-alert.

They are overly responsible.

They become hyperactive as a way of avoiding feelings.

They can be very judgmental and perfectionistic.

They display distorted thinking.

They have low self-esteem.

C. Attachment

While the terms "addiction" and "codependency" derive from psychology, "attachment" is used primarily in the area of spirituality.

In the twentieth century, psychology has contributed immensely to our understanding of the human person. Although many spiritual writers throughout history give evidence of a basic intuition of certain pivotal insights of modern psychology, they did not possess the scientific information available today. They lacked comprehension, for example, of predictable stages of human development; of family systems theory; of addiction as a disease; of methods for identifying and treating personality disorders. Therefore, most masters of Christian spirituality understood "attachment" as any fixation upon a creature, which fixation impedes a pilgrim's spiritual journey. That understanding would include, then, what we recognize today as addiction and codependency.

In light of current psychological insight, however, we believe it useful to distinguish attachment from addiction and codependency. Attachment in this more restricted sense marks the beginning of a process of fixing one's desire upon a person, object or situation in such a way as to make it a god. If unchecked, attachment can become addiction. In fact, every addiction begins with some form of attachment, and recovery from the addiction cannot attain completeness until the person sufficiently confronts the attachment.

Attachment — like addiction and codependency, but to a lesser degree — entails a distorted relationship, a mood-altering experience and some life-damaging effects.

Attached individuals set their hearts on a person, object or event in a twisted way. They seek from the creature something that he, she or it is incapable of giving. They cling possessively to the desired person or object, chasing a dream of living happily ever after.

That clinging provides, at least at the outset of the relationship, a mood-altering experience. It numbs some of the pain of the real life situation and provides a euphoric feeling, an ecstatic sensation, an emotional high. Engrossed enjoyment of the pleasure and incessant craving for its recurrence become a means of avoiding reality.

Any relationship based on attachment has life-damaging effects to the extent that it draws the person toward isolation and away from true intimacy with self, God, others and creation.

One distinction between attachment and addiction is found in a person's capacity for change. With awareness of the fixation and a genuine desire to recover, attached persons ordinarily have the capacity to take effective action. Their will is still functional enough to translate positive desire into action, provided they are disposed to suffer the consequences. Addicts, on the other hand, are powerless over their addiction. In saying that they want to change and in claiming that they can quit whenever they choose, they lie not only to others but to themselves. Addiction, by definition, means loss of the will-power necessary for change. The principle of recovery must come from a Power-greater-than-the-addict.

D. Common Characteristics

While addiction, codependency and attachment have their distinguishing characteristics, they share certain common qualities.

All three are based on relationships in which there exists some degree of emotional dependency upon a person, a thing or an activity. Addicted, codependent and attached persons use someone or something to evade pain and to replace it with pleasure. They fix on a creature in order to escape a feeling of powerlessness and to create a sense of control.

If we view attachment and addiction as the two extremes of a continuum, then we notice that the difference between them is primarily one of degree. Frequently, only fine lines separate the pathological relationship, the mood-alteration and the life-damaging consequences of an attachment from those of an addiction.

People may be at different levels of fixation in an addictive, a codependent or an attached process. Yet, despite those variations the acting-out follows a common cycle of preoccupation, ritualization, compulsive behavior and despair.

Preoccupation. Addicted, codependent and attached people become obsessed with the desired object. The preoccupation takes on a trance-like quality. They have run-away feelings and thoughts about what they want. Their obsession prevents them from focusing on the work at hand. The more they grow preoccupied, the more they lose connection with the real.

Ritualization. These persons engage in certain routines or rituals which intensify the preoccupation and constitute steps toward full engagement in the mood-altering experience.

Compulsive Behavior. The preoccupation and the ritualization finally augment to a point where addicted, codependent and attached persons act out their fixation. They let go the last vestiges of resistance and fully indulge.

At this point in the dynamic, a fundamental difference between addicts and attached persons comes into play. The former are overcome by their compulsivity. The latter are not compulsive in the technical sense. While retaining their power to resist, these choose to indulge.

Despair. Acting-out the compulsion or desire affords momentary relief. Since it does not last, that respite gives way to a realization that the fix is no longer working. Feelings of disgust, despair, guilt, shame and self-hatred take over. Those feelings in turn fuel the process. In order to escape this new pain the person must begin recreating the mood-altering experience. Thus, a vicious circle is created which quickly becomes a vortex.

In the case of addiction or codependency, each acting-out leaves the person more powerless to resist reenacting the preoccupation, ritualization, compulsive behavior and despair cycle. In the case of attachment, the individual still retains the potential willpower to change, the awareness of options and the capacity to choose otherwise. However, each acting-out causes some erosion of those qualities. Each indulgence is another step toward addiction.

CHAPTER 2

FAMILY SYSTEMS

Addiction, codependency and attachment arise from a person's disordered desires. However, that disorderedness is by no means a private affair. It directly impacts families, friends and associates. Indeed, it affects society itself.

Our society has many life-affirming values: freedom, caring, democracy, etc. Out of concern for its citizens, the general public holds certain behaviors as unbecoming: casual use of addictive drugs, heavy drinking, smoking to the disturbance of others, hard-core pornography, prostitution, gambling, etc. A number of those activities involve even legal consequences.

Yet, society fosters attitudes which have life-damaging repercussions. In some instances, the public and the addictive personality become partners in collusion in the sense that what a portion of society proposes as desirable in effect encourages compulsive behavior. Examples include: widespread sanction of climbing to the top whatever it takes, always being "number one," having a perfect body, amassing untold wealth, buying everything one wants whether one can afford it or needs it, constantly seeking quick results, maintaining control at practically any cost. Those drives create pressures which dispose even the strong-willed toward addiction and codependency.

The family is a microcosm of the culture and subcultures

in which it exists. A given family carries within its bosom a blend of national culture, ethnic background and, frequently, religious affiliation. Society values family life as both a mirror and the foundation of itself. Yet, the public also affirms as healthy certain modes of conjugal relationship and child-raising which are in effect dysfunctional. Thus, society and families too act as partners in collusion. The result of that collaboration is a style of family life which breeds addiction and codependency.

Addiction and codependency can occur in people who have come from healthy families of origin. The tragic death of a spouse or a sudden business collapse may tempt almost anyone to seek relief through substance abuse. Moreover, there is evidence that some people have a genetic predisposition toward intolerance of alcohol or certain chemicals.

However, most counselors and therapists agree that virtually every addict or codependent person comes from a family which is dysfunctional in some respect. Statistics indicate that growing up in such dysfunctionality puts the individual at high risk for addiction and codependency. In many instances, the compulsive behavior begins as a way of surviving in the family of origin.

The process of recovery from addiction or codependency begins with cessation of the compulsive behavior. The drinking must stop. The pills have to go. The effort to control everyone and everything must be relinquished. Breaking the addictive cycle is an essential first step. Recovery, however, does not stop there. While continuing to abstain from the addiction — or continuing to be moderate, as in the case of food, sex or a relationship — recovery requires that addicts and codependents get in touch with and work through their original pain.

For that reason, we focus in this chapter on family systems.

As for attachment, everyone has to struggle with that issue whether one comes from a functional or a dysfunctional family.

A. *Family as System*

By family system, we understand a group of blood-related persons interacting with one another. As a system, a family is more than the sum of the individuals which constitute it. It is not just a husband, a wife and children. A family as system is two spouses together with their children interrelating in such a way that each affects everyone else, as well as the balance of the whole.

A family system operates like a mobile hanging in a room. The mobile is made up of many pieces tenuously held in balance. Each part functions in relation to every other and to the mobile as a unit. Touch one piece and all the components are affected. They interrelate. They interconnect. One stir causes many adjusting moves so that the whole mobile can regain its equilibrium.

The primary relationship in a family system is fourfold: (1) the wife's relationship with herself and (2) with her husband; (3) the husband's relationship with himself and (4) with his wife. If both the husband and the wife experience meaningful self-intimacy and share a vibrant mutual relationship, an atmosphere exists where familial togetherness and personal differentiation are possible. That family system will be functional. If, however, self-intimacy is lacking or the marital relationship is unduly strained, a milieu exists in which all other family members will have to adapt to the dysfunctionality.

Each member of a family system is like a corporate personality. Each is both a unique person and an embodiment of the system. I am my individual self. Yet, I am in a sense also my family.

Like other systems, families can be closed or open. In dysfunctional contexts, the structures, the connections and the relationships are prescribed and rigid. In functional families, they are spontaneous and flexible.

Feedback — i.e., reactions to one another — determines

whether the family system is maintaining its usual patterns and processes or whether it is moving in the direction of change. Both maintenance and mutation can be either positive or negative. For instance, maintaining clear communication in interactions contributes to the system's effectiveness. On the other hand, perpetuating a cycle of actions that cover up addiction creates dysfunction. Change in a pattern enhances the system when directed toward growth. Variance is for the worst when it marks a regression from healthy modes of interaction.

A functional family system welcomes interrelatedness with other social systems. It values encounters with perspectives and convictions different from its own. It allows them to influence it. A dysfunctional family system, on the contrary, closes in upon itself. It tries to hide its dark secrets. It cuts itself off from sources which could provide corrective experiences.

Any family system has basic needs, for example: security; a sense of worth; productivity; unity; responsibility; physical, emotional and spiritual well-being. Roles in a family revolve around meeting those needs. Thus, various members play the part of hero, scapegoat, mascot, caretaker, clown, fairy godmother, little prince, martyr, super-achiever, etc. In a functional family system, every member has opportunities to try out many roles. In a dysfunctional system, however, each individual becomes locked into one or several roles.

B. Family Rules

The phrase "family rules" denotes repeated patterns of interaction observable within a family unit. Each family rule embodies attitudes, behaviors and consequences of behavior. Those patterns of interaction may be explicit or implicit. They develop in reference to the various aspects of family life: finances, socialization, sex, education, religion, etc.

(1) *In Functional Family Systems*

Generally, the following patterns of interaction occur in a healthy family:

> The family system is at the service of the individual and not vice versa.
>
> Each member has the freedom to express his/her perceptions, thoughts, feelings, desires and dreams.
>
> Individual needs are adequately met.
>
> Members feel close, while each one strives to develop a separate identity.
>
> There is effective communication, based on the concrete, specific and behavioral aspects of family life.
>
> Problems and difficulties are openly acknowledged and specifically resolved.
>
> Each parent develops clearly defined ego boundaries, and teaches the children to do the same.
>
> In disciplinary matters, the parents are consistent, just and self-disciplined.
>
> Personal responsibility and accountability are required of each member — parents included.
>
> Members have permission to make mistakes in their growth process.
>
> Members exercise forgiveness and seek reconciliation when hurt occurs.

(2) *In Dysfunctional Family Systems*

Meanwhile, the following principles usually underlie the distressful interaction of a dysfunctional family. These rules ordinarily operate covertly and without conscious awareness. Yet they affect to varying degrees each member of the system:

> Always be in control of all interaction and behavior, or you will be victimized.

Always be right and do the right thing, or you will be
squelched.

Don't talk about your feelings, your needs or your concerns, for they will be ignored or ridiculed.

Deny your perceptions, thoughts, feelings, desires,
fantasies, lest you no longer fit in with the rest of
the family.

If things don't turn out as you planned, blame someone —
either yourself or someone else.

Always be on the alert for the unpredictable, because you
never know what's going to happen next.

Don't depend on anyone to fulfill your needs, so that you
will not be constantly disappointed.

Keep the same fights going, because in order to resolve
differences you have to be vulnerable — and to be
vulnerable causes you to be hurt over and over
again.

C. The Poisonous Pedagogy

Among the family rules, certain ones define the core of
parent-child interaction. The cultural and subcultural group-
ings in which new families form have a collective way of
believing, seeing and appraising behavior. That collective
outlook is commonly referred to as "consensus reality" or
"conventional thinking." Children and many adults assume
that viewpoint in a noncritical and nonreflective way. Thus
they live, act and react according to the generally accepted
patterns and rules of society.

Until recent decades, the consensus reality dominating
family life among Western peoples has been what Alice Miller,
a pioneer in this field, calls "the poisonous pedagogy."[1] The
basic tenets of that model of parent-child interaction are as
follows:

1. See *Select Bibliography*.

Adults are the masters of the child who is dependent on
them for everything.

Adults determine in godlike fashion what is right and
wrong.

The child is held responsible for the parents' anger.

Parents must always be shielded.

The child's life-affirming feelings pose a threat to the
autocratic adult.

The child's will must be "broken" as soon as possible.

All this must happen at a very early age, so that the child
"won't notice" what is taking place, and will
therefore not be able to expose the adults.

Integral to that poisonous pedagogy are the following false
information and distorted beliefs which are passed on by
parents to children, from generation to generation:

Duty and compliance produce love.

Hatred can be abolished by forbidding it.

Parents deserve servile respect simply because they are
parents.

Children are undeserving of basic human respect simply
because they are children.

Blind obedience makes a child strong.

Too much self-esteem is harmful.

Low self-esteem makes a person altruistic.

Tenderness — often viewed as doting — is harmful.

Responding to a child's needs is wrong.

Severity and coldness are a good preparation for life.

Pretense of gratitude is better than honest ingratitude.

The way you behave is more important than the way you
really are.

Neither parents nor God could survive being offended.

The body is dirty and disgusting.

Strong feelings are harmful.

Parents are free of drives and guilt.

Parents are always right.

Parent-child interaction based on such poisonous pedagogy is clearly abusive. Because of the loss of self which is experienced by parents and children alike, family systems governed by the above rules invite addiction, codependency and attachment.

D. Toward Change in "Conventional Thinking"

While today perhaps only a minority of parents would accept outright the tenets of the poisonous pedagogy, mitigated versions of that style of parenting still abound. Estimates that between 80-95% of families in the United States are dysfunctional testify to that alarming fact.

Nonetheless, as the twenty-first century dawns, consciousness of the damaging effects of the poisonous pedagogy is spreading far and wide. Many fathers and mothers are trying to create more compassionate and dialogical styles of raising their children. These parents do not acknowledge as values blind obedience, coercion and denial of feelings. They seek to respect the innate dignity and unique individuality of their children.

Yet in pursuing those goals, many parents become blocked by a need to deny or to repress the pain of their own childhood. To be empathetic toward their children, they have to embrace their own wounded inner child. To avoid using and abusing their children, they must courageously face their own original pain. To be able to listen to their children, they have to be aware of their own interior truth. Otherwise, despite good intentions and sincere efforts, these parents too will pass on to another generation the violence inflicted upon them.

Many adults do not even know what happened to them in childhood. They are not consciously aware of the violence that befell them in their family of origin. They accept as normal and healthy what was abusive and damaging. Idealization of their parents and avoidance of pain still prevent them from recognizing the truth. As long as they persist in that stance, they teeter on the brink of addiction, codependency and attachment.

CHAPTER 3

THE ORIGINAL TRAUMA: ABANDONMENT

Each of us is born into a family system which functions as an organism with its own patterns of interaction. Roles, needs and rules already exist. From infancy through childhood on into adolescence, we feel our way into the system. Ordinarily, we grow into our place within the family in a noncritical and nonreflective manner. We do not even realize that we are part of a system, let alone question it. Moreover, we assume for a long time that every other family operates like our own, for we have no other experience by which to judge. Thus we participate in our family system as if a spell were cast over us.

If we are to mature, however, the spell must be broken. With the onset of adulthood — if not already in adolescence — many of our illusions begin to dissipate. Separation from our parents requires that we realistically assess our family of origin. We have to consider it from an observer's viewpoint, so to speak. Sifting through a myriad of influences, we form a personalized value system and our own set of convictions. These are sometimes quite different from those of our family and society.

That process is integral to human development. Yet denied or repressed pain pertaining to our early years can obstruct its natural unfolding. Most of us take for granted that life in our family of origin was healthy. Yet we do not really know whether our family system was functional or dysfunctional until we critically examine it. If we did grow up in a dysfunctional system, it is highly probable that we carry within us much pain and hurt.

The trauma that befalls many people in their family of origin is abandonment.

A. *Abandonment*

Abandonment means that as children we were left on our own, left out or left to fend for ourselves. Our parents were not consistently present to us in a way that sufficiently affirmed our needs, affects and drives. Abandonment in that sense occurs not only in families where there is blatant addiction but also in families where parents appear kind and devoted.

Every child experiences moments when parents fail to listen and to understand. That is a normal part of growing up. For many of us as children, however, that unavailability became an habitual, predictable pattern of interaction. Repeated incidents eventually accumulated to a point where we developed an ongoing feeling of abandonment and began enacting survival strategies. Some people can identify a specific incident which symbolizes the rupture in their relationship with their parents. Others cannot. Whether we have only a general sense of abandonment or a consciousness of a personal history leading up to a significant wounding, our childhood trauma was compounded by the fact that we were unable to express our suffering. We had to repress it. We stuffed the pain away, deep inside ourselves.

Until we acknowledge and work through that hurt, it colors our lives. The original trauma is like a lens through which we view the world and interpret events. We have to own our past if we are to wrestle free from its grip. We must attend to our wounded inner child if we are to stop pursuing in our adult relationships what was denied us as children.

Examining our family system is a way to connect with and

to experience the pain of our original trauma. Perceiving family as system, however, means recognizing that the fault does not necessarily lie with our parents but with the system itself. It is the rules, the rituals and the roles that have been passed on from generation to generation which wreak havoc. We need to know our family system in order to understand what happened to us. That first step opens the way to breaking the cycle of violence and to choosing healthy patterns of interaction.

B. Catalysts for Abandonment

Each person's experience of abandonment is unique. Yet one or a combination of three factors frequently sets the dynamic in motion. They are: physical absence, narcissistic deprivation and abuse in one form or another.

(1) Physical Absence

A parent may simply walk out on a family, never to be seen or heard from again. A parent may become permanently absent through death. Separation or divorce causes its own kind of division between parent and child. Addiction, with its preoccupations, rituals and acting out, distances a parent from every member of the system.

Because young children's thinking is egocentric and magical, they tend to surmise that physical absence results somehow from their badness or unworthiness.

(2) Narcissistic Deprivation

Mirroring and echoing by parents provide self-affirmation to young children who need to be seen and respected as unique individuals as well as the central actors in their activity. Although narcissistic, the fulfillment of that need is essential to a child's burgeoning sense of self-love and self-esteem.

When young children have experienced respect for their feelings, needs and drives, they are well prepared to move from a symbiotic relationship with parents to a stance of autonomy and independence.

However, many parents were themselves narcissistically deprived in their early years. No one or no thing can ever give them what they missed at the appropriate time in their development. Yet, without realizing the origin of their craving, those adults long for someone who will take care of them and fulfill their every wish. Narcissistically deprived parents tend to direct that longing toward their children.

From birth, children intuit narcissistic deprivation in their parents. Sensing that they are utterly dependent on their parents for survival, they do all in their power to avoid losing them. To that end, they conform to their parents' narcissistic expectations of them. They try to be and to act according to their parents' every whim. In an effort to secure parental love, they parent their parents, so to speak. That reversal of roles constitutes a form of abandonment, since the child's personality, needs and feelings are in effect disregarded.

Parents who are narcissistically deprived tend to neglect other dependency needs in their growing children, like:

the need for safety;
the need for a trustworthy relationship;
the need to be held and touched;
the need to belong;
the need for autonomy;
the need for boundaries and structures;
the need for guidance.

Neglect of dependency needs leads to the following problems in children:

inability to trust their own emotions;
absence of the emotional development which results from trial and error experiences;
lack of a sense of their true needs;
intense alienation from self.

Under those circumstances, children cannot emancipate themselves from their parents. Even as adults, they remain dependent on affirmation from their partners, from society and especially from their own children. Thus narcissistic deprivation is handed down from generation to generation.

(3) *Abuse*

Abuse can be physical, sexual, verbal, emotional, mental.

A child experiences all forms of abuse by a parent as abandonment. In using the child to act out unresolved conflicts or frustrations, the parent is incapable of responding to the child's needs and feelings. Abuse is a violation of the child's dignity and human rights. It is a negation of his/her inner self.

In some instances, while not the direct recipients of abuse, children witness abuse of a parent or a sibling; for example, a father beating the mother or screaming uncontrollably at an older brother. As witnesses to the abuse, those children too are victims of the violence. They are left with feelings of powerlessness and horror. They linger in trepidation, wondering when the ax will strike them.

Abused children learn from their parents low impulse control and mistrust of people. They carry with them into adulthood excruciating pain. Many perpetuate in their new families the violence that was inflicted upon them in childhood. Abuse, too, can be passed on from generation to generation.

C. *Internalized Shame*

For an experience of abandonment to occur in traumatic fashion, three factors ordinarily preexist: an interpersonal relationship, a basic trust and a certain sense of security.

Specific instances of sudden abandonment happen in every parent-child relationship. Parents cannot always foresee

the impact their behavior will have. Neither can they always
control the circumstances in which they act. At times, a child
will feel alienation as a result of a well-intentioned correction,
a necessary absence of a parent or a simple oversight. When
that happens, the child's basic expectations of the parent are
suddenly exposed as wrong. The unexpected betrayal by the
trusted parent exposes the child's self to view. The child feels
inferior, unworthy, not good enough. In a word, the child
experiences shame.

Ordinarily, parents can mend a breach of an interpersonal bond with a child by being vulnerable, by recognizing the child's true need, by acknowledging that need to the
child and, if applicable, by admitting the violation of trust.
That course of action usually restores intimacy, even when the
parent chooses not to gratify the child.

Many children, however, are abandoned repeatedly by
their parents, without any consistent effort to restore intimacy.
When emotional severing occurs time and again, the child's
shame evolves into a persistent state of being. The situation is
no longer: "I *feel* shame." It has become: "I *am* shameful."
Thus, shame is internalized. It infiltrates the child's self-
identity.

Shame as a feeling can be positive. For example, a
healthy sense of shame balances the emerging autonomy of a
child between the ages of fifteen months and three years.
Healthy shame indicates limitations. It teaches us when we are
playing God by attempting to transgress those boundaries.
Healthy shame delineates the parameters of power and giftedness. It prods us to seek appropriate assistance. It reminds us
that we are human, and invites us to value our humanity. In
adulthood, healthy shame is associated with prudence and
circumspection.

On the other hand, the internalized shame which results
from abandonment is destructive. When shame becomes integral to our self-identity, we feel defective as human beings.
We see ourselves as radically flawed, inadequate, worthless.
Moreover, we envisage no way out of our defectiveness. We

sense that nothing can be done to correct our worthlessness.

While the underlying dynamic remains the same, the conscious experience of internalized shame varies from person to person. Some experience it in terms of vague or explicit feelings of emptiness, unlovability, rejection. Others experience it as persistent self-doubt, guilt, inadequacy.

Children who feel abandoned and who have internalized shame formulate tragic core beliefs about themselves:

> I am a bad person.
> I am unworthy of being loved by God or by another human being.
> I will be abandoned by any person who cares for me.
> I cannot depend on anyone to fulfill my needs.

Over time, those beliefs recede into the child's unconscious. There they acquire even more power to undermine self-love and self-esteem.

Internalized shame can bind not only self-identity but also the child's emotions, needs and drives. For instance, if anger arises, I am ashamed of my anger. If I need to be held, I feel shame at my dependency. If I experience genital curiosity, I become ashamed of my sexuality.

As long as internalized shame persists, feelings of shame can arise without external stimuli. A shame-bound child activates shame spontaneously from within. For example, simple awareness of a limitation or a failure is enough to catapult the child into a terrifying sense of inadequacy as a human being.

Internalized shame also disposes a child to be swept up into a shame spiral. For instance, a triggering event occurs which causes the child to think that s/he will be abandoned again by a significant person. The child goes into a tail-spin. Thoughts and feelings of shame swirl uncontrollably. A vicious circle commences as the child dwells on the triggering episode, reliving it over and over again. Engulfed in the escalating spiral, the child loses all sight of more affirming feelings.

Any child with healthy self-esteem finds painful the

sudden exposure of self which occurs in abandonment by a parent. But children with internalized shame — and hence low self-esteem — find unexpected exposure utterly intolerable. These children already see themselves as unlovable and un-worthy. Therefore, they believe that to be exposed is to be seen in all their defectiveness as human beings.

Abandonment of one form or another is the trauma that numerous people undergo in early life. For many of us that experience was heightened by additional factors. We were not allowed to discuss our suffering. We were told that what we felt happening was not in fact occurring. We were taught that what was causing violence to us was in effect good. Through it all, our inner woundedness persisted, and we were left increas-ingly ashamed of ourselves.

CHAPTER 4

THE COVER-UP:
SELF DIVIDED AGAINST SELF

Abandonment and internalized shame left many of us in ex-cruciating pain during childhood. We became emotional or-phans. Such relentless suffering could not, however, be long tolerated in its raw state.

As children, we so identified with our parents that we learned to see ourselves as they saw us. The traits and be-haviors which met with their approval, we were inclined to develop. Those which they rejected, we tended to avoid. In an effort to be acceptable to our parents, we split off and hid away the aspects of our personality which they would not affirm. Thus self became divided against itself.

Through it all, we nonetheless maintained some connec-tion with our true self. A certain degree of unique identity and vibrant life persisted. For some, that connectedness was weak, like an ember; for others, it was fairly strong, like a flame.

Yet as abandoned children we became in varying degrees runaways from our true self. We hid our inmost being not only from our parents but also from ourselves. We avoided our shame-based identity, and tried to prevent its further exposure to ourselves and to anyone else. We evaded our inner pain and attempted to prevent any more suffering from befalling us. Gradually, we came to hide from our hiding, to avoid our avoidance. As our true self became more distant, we developed a new stance to present to the world: a mask, a persona, an impersonator, a false self.

The strategies we employed to achieve and to perpetuate that cover-up are called defense mechanisms.

A. Defense Mechanisms

Defense mechanisms are adaptations used for survival. They are means of coping with a reality that seems overwhelming or engulfing at the time it befalls us. They are strategies for dealing with the pain resulting from circumstances, events or people that either intentionally or unintentionally hurt us. Defense mechanisms are protections against threats to our existence.

Human beings have available to them a vast repertoire of defense mechanisms. Some are instinctive, like repression. Others are learned, like operating out of a life script.

Defense mechanisms are not always harmful. They can serve a useful purpose, provided we let them go when the proper time arrives. During trauma, defense mechanisms ensure survival. They protect the individual from what is too much to bear all at once. Certain defense mechanisms — like temporary role playing and some acting-out behaviors — can be constructive ways of protecting our personal boundaries. They help us assert our rights to privacy, to respect, to human dignity. In daily life, awareness of our defending strategies and conscious choice to use or not to use them are signs of healthy adaptation.

Those of us, however, who grew up in dysfunctional family systems and who carry unresolved abandonment issues tend to overuse defense mechanisms. Since those strategies ensured survival during childhood and adolescence, we continue as adults to employ them as our basic mode of relating. Since those defenses are so familiar to us — almost second nature — we see them as normal patterns of interaction. All memory of our early trauma may have receded from consciousness. Yet we continue to rely on old coping strategies. Our false self thus becomes reinforced, and we remain alienated from our true identity.

In the rest of this chapter, we describe the most common adaptations to the trauma of abandonment and its shaming effects. No individual is likely to use all of them, nor will they be experienced in exactly the same way by any two persons. Genetic and environmental factors, as well as the behaviors most favored in a family system, influence greatly the choice of adaptive strategies.

B. Primary Ego Defenses

The primary ego defense system is automatic and unconscious. It is instinctively activated when we encounter a severe threat. Among the primary ego defenses which children employ in the experience of abandonment are the following: fantasy bonding, repression, projection, dissociation, displacement, depersonalization, conversion and identification.

(1) Fantasy Bonding

Fantasy bonding is an adaptation whereby the child denies that the trauma is occurring and creates an illusion of connectedness with the abandoning and shaming parents.

Children are dependent upon their parents for survival. The thought of being all alone without anyone genuinely caring is unbearable. Therefore, when abandonment occurs, children idealize their parents and assume the blame themselves. The child's attitude toward the parent is this: "It can't be your fault, so it must be mine." "You can do no wrong; so there must be something wrong with me."

(2) Repression

Repression is a process by which children exclude from consciousness unacceptable feelings, needs or drives and relegate them to the unconscious. The child shuts down emotionally so as not to feel pain. Repression is an emotional numb-out.

(3) *Projection*

By projection, children attribute to other people feelings, ideas or qualities which in reality are their own. For example: If I deny how frightened I am, I may read you as afraid.

Omnipotence is a dimension of the young child's egocentricity which becomes projected on parents. Seeing the parents as god-like reinforces the abandoned child's belief: "You can't be the problem; I must be."

(4) *Dissociation*

Some children cope with abandonment by splitting off their feelings from the event. Dissociation is thus a severing of the link between the trauma and the response to it. For instance, a child being physically abused may leave the body by becoming mentally spaced out.

(5) *Displacement*

Once dissociation occurs, displacement generally follows. That is, the blocked memory of the event and the feelings associated with it are usually placed elsewhere. Frequently this takes the form of recurring nightmares or flights of fantasy.

(6) *Depersonalization*

The child in being abandoned no longer sees him/herself as a vibrant human being but as a discarded object. This ego defense causes a loss of contact with the inner world of experience. The child loses feeling-connectedness with the outer world as well.

(7) *Conversion*

Conversion is understood here not in its theological sense of a radical turning toward God, but rather in the psychological sense of a strategy for changing a shameful or forbidden feeling, need or drive into another that is more tolerable. A child may convert anger, for example, into guilt or fear. An adolescent may convert the need for intimacy into sexual activity.

(8) *Identification*

The abandoned child might identify with the parent as a victim would with an aggressor. In so doing, the child evades feelings of helplessness and shame by feeling powerful like the parent. A victim who identifies with an aggressor tends to behave aggressively toward other people.

C. *Other Defenses*

As children grow older, they erect other layers of defenses to cover up abandonment and shame and to protect themselves against further abuse. Ordinarily, defenses like role playing, acting-out behaviors and life scripts are more deliberately enacted and consciously fostered than the primary ego defenses.

(1) *Roles*

The roles we play can be a healthy means of interaction provided that:

We remain in touch with our true self.
We have some awareness that we are playing a part.
We choose the role.
We engage in it on a temporary basis.
We can switch roles when adaptation requires it.

Abandoned children — and adults who have not resolved their abandonment issues — overidentify with both societal and familial roles. For instance, a boy conforms to society's idea of the masculine. He becomes the macho male who rejects the vulnerable aspects of himself. A girl becomes fixated in the role of the helpless female who refuses to own her inner strength and to take a personal stand. In family life, a child becomes locked into the role of super-achiever or surrogate spouse.

Because identification with roles creates a certain security and predictability, children can temporarily avoid their abandonment and internalized shame. Over time, however, that identification causes further shame, because it increases alienation from one's true self.

(2) *Acting-out Behavior*

Acting-out behaviors include: rage, contempt, perfectionism, quest for power and control, blame and criticism, judgmentalism, arrogance, envy, caretaking, pleasing others, rescuing.

People use those coping devices to ward off shame once it has occurred. They try to lessen their own shame by transferring it to another.

(3) *Life Scripts*

Instead of focusing on discovering and actualizing their inner direction, some people who have experienced abandonment tend to live according to someone else's script.

That script usually evolves in the family of origin. It can be explicit or implicit. It consists of a set of expectations that parents or siblings have for a member. Life scripts set up what the person is to be and to do. For example, one child may be expected to be a priest or a nun. Another is supposed to marry a certain type of person, live close to home and have two children: a boy and a girl. Still another child's script may designate him/her as the one who will never amount to anything.

Living according to a life script is a way of evading inner pain. It is a means of remaining connected with significant persons at the expense of one's real self. It is not that the life direction is necessarily wrong. The difficulty rather lies in the individual's lack of freedom and conscious choice of that lifestyle. It is as if the person had been preprogrammed into it.

D. Addiction: A Last Resort

Those of us who grow up hiding our true self behind layer upon layer of coping strategies live in unbearable chronic pain. To the misery of our original trauma, we add the suffering of living defensively. We are alienated from ourselves, from others, from God. We persist in intolerable loneliness, desperate to find even fleeting relief. We search for something — anything — to take away the hurt. Eventually, many of us are reduced to the final defense against our excruciating anguish: addiction.

Whatever soothes our suffering is potentially addictive — a substance, a person, a relationship, an activity. If we go the course of addiction, that object becomes an all-consuming purpose in life. We will run with rapidly increasing frequency to the source of mood-alteration because our pain is unrelenting. We will rationalize, deny or manipulate; beg, borrow or steal; deceive, cheat or lie to protect that source. Relating with the object of addiction becomes the pivotal experience in our life. We are then powerless to stop ourselves. Our life is out of control. We move further away from our true self, and further decrease our intimacy with God and others.

Addiction is the last resort in trying to cover up pain. Yet, like all other defense mechanisms, it serves only to increase suffering and shame. Addiction is life-damaging and life-threatening. If it progresses unchecked, it will kill.

CHAPTER 5

RECOVERY

Throughout this section, we have described from primarily a psychological perspective the inner woundedness of most addicted, codependent and attached persons.

However, those of us who carry that pain are not doomed to it forever. Healing is possible. We can be set free. We can let go. We can reclaim our true self. We can enter the process of recovery from addiction, codependency and attachment.

A. *Recovery as Process*

All that is human in us seeks naturally and spontaneously to be whole.

Recovery then means opening ourselves to the life force which wells up from within our inmost being.

Recovery, moreover, denotes returning to life, discovering a new zest for life, becoming a life-giving person.

Recovery, furthermore, implies learning to better love ourselves, other persons, creation and God. It connotes letting ourselves receive love.

Recovery ultimately is a spiritual awakening.

Recovery from addiction, codependency or attachment occurs for the most part in the context of the ordinary ebb and flow of daily existence. It happens through healthy involvement in relationships, work and leisure. The recovery process is usually slow and painstaking. It requires commitment, patience and perseverance. It demands investment of much time and energy.

The recovery process thrusts us toward healing. It restores in us the integrity we had lost. It directs us toward reclaiming our unique identity. Yet, recovery entails not only rediscovery of our authentic self but also its development. Recovery guides us toward the full actualization of who we are.

From a Christian standpoint, recovery extends far beyond self-discovery and self-actualization. Recovery ultimately includes re-creation of the whole person by God:

> If anyone is in Christ,
>   s/he is a new creation.
> The old order has passed away:
>   Behold! an entirely new order has come.
> All this is God's work (2 Cor 5:17-18).

Recovery in that sense converges on and becomes integral to the process of transforming union:

> We who with unveiled faces contemplate the glory of God
>   are being transformed in his image,
>   progressing from glory to glory.
> This is the work of the Lord (2 Cor 3:18).

That transformation in God, by God, implies much purgation and purification — hence, productive suffering — as the next two sections of this book will highlight.

B. The Initial Moment of Truth

Entrance into recovery is marked by consciousness of the reality of addiction, codependency or attachment. The truth of our condition becomes undeniable. Our eyes open to the excruciating pain we are inflicting upon ourselves. We catch a glimpse of how deeply we are hurting those we love. We feel acutely our alienation from self, other persons and God. We face head-on the emptiness, the dreadfulness, the meaning-lessness of our existence. We admit that our lives are unmanageable.

Each addicted, codependent or attached person experi-ences a unique providential turn of events which brings him/her to that initial moment of truth. Yet there are certain common circumstances which frequently usher in the recovery process.

The providential turning point may have been another's sharing of a personal struggle with addiction. Something from a class, a seminar or a video may have struck us like a ton of bricks. Perhaps it was a book that fell our way at just the right time. Maybe we were shocked into admitting the disastrous effects of actions like causing a car wreck, seeing our children go hungry because we squandered the family income on our addiction, or finding that a trusted friend has given up on us. We may have arrived home one day only to discover an "intervention" waiting on the doorstep — our family and friends standing together and confronting us regarding our behavior. Their tough love approach may have jolted us into reality.

Paradoxically, the intensity of our pain is itself the most effective catalyst for recovery. Many of us hit rock-bottom before we come to our senses (Lk 15:13-17). That experience takes sundry shapes: physical collapse, termination of em-ployment, divorce, separation, bankruptcy, etc. For others, the externals of life may be manageable still, but they feel like they have reached a dead end.

Thus, the increasing misery of maintaining an addiction, codependency or attachment eventually outweighs the original pain which we are trying to escape. We conclude that avoid-ance is no longer worth the cost. That soul-wrenching experi-ence puts a crack in our defense system. We become open enough at that moment to admit the truth of our condition and to begin in earnest the inner journey toward personal transformation.

C. The Recovery Process

In reaction to the original trauma of abandonment, we constructed layer upon layer of avoidance mechanisms. We set up those coping strategies initially around our deepest self and then built gradually outward toward the most observable dimensions of personhood. In recovery, however, we proceed in reverse order. That is, we begin with the outermost layer of defenses and progress toward the core. While the impetus to seek healing springs from our deepest self, we start recovery at the behavioral level and move painstakingly inward to reclaim our true self.

The first step in healing is abstinence. We must abstain from the addictive object, person or situation as well as from the rituals leading up to the compulsive behavior. Some addictions require total abstinence: alcohol and drugs, for example. Others — such as food, money, work — call for moderation, since many of them are necessary for daily living.

Breaking the addictive cycle is an initial move toward reestablishment of intimacy with self, others, creation and God. That positive behavior modification enables self-intimacy by letting emotional numb-out give way to real feelings. In reaching out to God for healing and to trusted people for support, the recovering person starts fostering meaningful relationships.

Gradually, internalized shame becomes externalized. "I am shameful" turns into "I feel shame." That shift results from both personal honesty and affirmation from supportive people. As internalized shame is released, shame-bound feelings are also set free.

From recovery of our capacity to feel, we proceed to confront our false self with its roles, life scripts and acting-out behaviors. Going deeper, we work our way through the primary ego defense system to our true self.

The path through defense mechanisms is not straight and narrow. Even when we have torn down a layer of coping strategies, we need to be vigilant lest they be reactivated. The path is winding and hilly, punctuated with successes and failures, light and darkness, small victories and frustrating setbacks.

As we uncover our defenses, we confront our pain — both the suffering of our avoidance and the hurt of the original abandonment. The only productive way to deal with pain is to pass through it. Healing begins with feeling. We mourn. We grieve. We perceive our loss. We feel hopeless, confused, anxious at times. We encounter our attachments at every turn. Yet, in the dying process, a renewed self slowly emerges:

> Unless the grain of wheat falls to the ground and dies,
>   it remains only a single seed.
> But if it dies,
>   it bears fruit abundantly (Jn 12:24).

D. *Supports for Recovery*

Each person in recovery from addiction or codependency needs to establish a meaningful support system. Besides friends and loved ones, that support system can include: a new family of affiliation, attendance at workshops, appropriate reading material, individual therapy, group therapy, personal leisure and solitary prayer.

Many people in recovery find participation in a Twelve-Step Program especially valuable. Originally, that approach was developed for recovering alcoholics and adult children of alcoholics. In recent years, the twelve steps have been adapted for recovery from any form of addiction. They are:

1. We admitted that we are powerless over our addiction — that our lives have become unmanageable.
2. We came to believe that a Power-greater-than-ourselves could restore us to sanity.
3. We made a decision to turn our will and our lives over to the care of God as we understood God.

4. We made a searching and fearless moral inventory of ourselves.
5. We admitted to God, to ourselves and to another human being the exact nature of our wrongs.
6. We were entirely ready to have God remove all these defects of character.
7. We humbly asked God to remove our shortcomings.
8. We made a list of all persons we had harmed, and became willing to make amends to them all.
9. We made direct amends to such people wherever possible, except when to do so would injure them or others.
10. We continued to take personal inventory, and when we were wrong promptly admitted it.
11. We sought prayer and meditation to improve our conscious contact with God as we understood God, praying only for knowledge of his will for us and the power to carry it out.
12. Having had a spiritual awakening as a result of these steps, we tried to carry this message to others and to practice these principles in all our affairs.

E. Theological Underpinnings for Recovery

Whatever support system we use in recovery from addiction, codependency or attachment, a threefold movement is inescapable:

1. Letting go our desire for the fix as well as the fixation itself;
2. Confronting and working through pain, suffering and hurt;
3. A spiritual awakening wherein we are drawn into ever deeper intimacy with self, others, creation and God.

Both Eastern and Western mystics have consistently avowed that detachment is essential to authentic selfhood and communion with creation and God. Yet many people cringe at the thought of detachment because they associate it with negation of creatures or with self-abasement as an end in itself. Some dualistic and masochistic tendencies are undeniably evident in the history of spirituality. Nonetheless, true Christian detachment opens us to the freedom of the children of God. Detachment is a letting go of the egocentric desires which cause us to cling to someone or something.

Detachment does not in itself require removal of the person, situation or object from our life — except in the case of chemical dependency. Rather, detachment means learning to love as God loves and to be loved with God's own love. Authentic detachment does not lead to isolation or withdrawal from people or creation. Rather, it is a necessary inner attitude and condition for full enjoyment of all aspects of life. While detachment implies leaving all, it is for the purpose of returning to all in a transformed and purified relationship.

For the remainder of this book, we explore more specifically the mystery of Christian detachment. We address theological underpinnings for recovery from addiction, codependency and attachment. To facilitate that, we draw upon pertinent insights of St. John of the Cross (1542-1591) and Pierre Teilhard de Chardin (1881-1955).

For John of the Cross, detachment is a freedom of spirit which we receive as we pass through the dark night of the soul. John insists that every person, thing and event in our lives can have a positive yet purifying role in our transformation. Thus, the ultimate lesson of healthy involvement — as well as of unhealthy engrossment — with creation is that God alone fulfills the deepest yearnings of the human heart. God's loving presence, manifest in, through and beyond creation, wounds us with increasing desire for God in himself.

John emphasizes that undergoing the pain of personal purification and transformation in God is the only way to attain the consummated happiness to which we are called. To find our identity in Christ and to let God become all in all (1 Cor 15:28), we have to take up our cross daily (Lk 9:23). Yet that night is not punishment or even primarily expiation. The night pertains to the exigencies of divine love. It is thus a *blessed night*.

Pierre Teilhard de Chardin focuses on the pain integral to the evolutionary process — both the evolution of creation in general as well as the spiritual genesis of each person. What John terms "dark night" Teilhard refers to as the "passivities of existence," the "passivities of growth," the "passivities of diminishment" and "receptivity of a superior order." According to Teilhard, we recover and develop our transformed self through undergoing pain and suffering. Detachment, therefore, occurs by passing-all-the-way-through the created and by sublimation.

John gives considerable attention to the process of becoming free of existing attachments. Teilhard, for his part, stresses how we move forward on our spiritual journey by using creation as a positive support in our transformation.

Neither John nor Teilhard had available to him contemporary insights into addiction and codependency. Yet many aspects of the dark night and of the passivities provide insightful theological reflection on recovery from addition and codependency as well as from attachment.

ST. JOHN OF THE CROSS
ON DETACHMENT

CHAPTER 6

THE POSITIVE YET PURIFYING ROLE OF CREATURES IN OUR DIVINIZATION

Two characteristics of people entrapped by addictions, codependency and attachments are these: (1) They try to force the creatures in their lives to supply them with more happiness and completeness than creation can offer. They use creatures narcissistically. They abuse them. (2) Addicted, codependent and attached individuals also go to extremes to avoid pain. Yet, suffering and death — or what is frequently referred to as the dark night of the soul — are integral to human life and, therefore, cannot ultimately be evaded.

In order to recover, addicted, codependent and attached persons must, first, come to appreciate creation according to God's purpose and to use creatures positively on their spiritual journey. Second, addicted, codependent and attached people have to realize that pain, suffering and death can in faith have a constructive and providential role in life. One overcomes unavoidable pain not by deadening oneself against it, but by going through suffering and letting the Lord use it for good.

Those are the principal theological issues which we examine from complementary points of view: St. John of the Cross's understanding of detachment and Pierre Teilhard de Chardin's contribution of an evolutionary perspective to the question.

An element of doctrine seldom emphasized by commentaries on the Mystical Doctor[1] is the positive and perfecting role of creatures in our sanctification.

To discover John's teaching on the evangelical meaning and providential place of creation in the process of divinization, we turn to *The Spiritual Canticle*. Most of the stanzas of that poem were composed in 1578 during John's imprisonment by Calced Carmelite Friars in their attempt to strangle the Discalced reform within their order.

A. *Spiritual Canticle: Stanza 1*

The poem begins abruptly with the anxious cry of the soul in search of its Beloved:

> Where have you hidden yourself,
> O my Beloved, having left me in anguish?
> You fled like the deer,
> Having wounded me.
> I went forth searching frantically for you,
> and you were gone.

That initial stanza sets the tone for all that follows. When God opens our hearts more deeply to himself, we experience a painful wound of love. This wound becomes manifest in the agonizing realization that the Beloved has vanished without warning. Thus we experience ourselves drowning in an ever more obscure sea of confusion. We set out anxiously searching.

Previously, we had felt secure, self-confident and self-reliant. Divine consolations abounded. We were basking in the light of God's radiance. Then, suddenly and for no apparent reason, that whole world of divine enjoyment disappears. What we had naively assumed to have been God is not God at all. We experience ourselves lost, abandoned, alone.

---

1. Pope Pius XI proclaimed St. John of the Cross Doctor of the Universal Church in all things ascetical and mystical on August 24, 1926.

Meditation on those verses of the opening stanza of *The Spiritual Canticle* enables us to experience through a certain empathy some of the sentiments which must have passed through John's heart as he wasted away during his confinement. Also transparent in those verses are the lineaments of the interior journey of each of us in the course of our deification.

(1) *Hidden by Reason of Transcendence*

"Where have you hidden yourself, O my Beloved?" That is: "O Word, my Spouse, show me the place where you are concealed." In that prayer, we ask God "for the manifestation of his divine essence, because the place where the Son of God is hidden . . . is the bosom of the Father . . . which is concealed from mortal eyes and shrouded from every form of human understanding."[2]

In that way, divine *transcendence* constitutes the first source of the pain of absence. The deeper the Lord draws us into loving communion with himself, the more we are forced to acknowledge that he completely transcends all we can ever know or experience of him. God so surpasses our powers of perceiving, understanding and feeling that we are left in a state of panic. The Lord seems far away.

The pain of that realization is intensified by the fact that up to this threshold of interiorization, we had felt so intimately close to God. Now, at least on a sensory level, all has changed. Moreover, we fear that the change may be for the worst.

(2) *Hidden within the Intimate Being of the Soul*

John does not, however, belabor the fact of God's transcendence in this context. That truth should be evident to every pilgrim. He emphasizes instead the other essential — yet rarely accentuated — element of doctrine: namely, the paradoxical experience of the absence of God by reason of his *immanence.*

---

2. *Canticle*, 1, 3.

> The Word, together with the Father and the Spirit, is
> hidden in essence and in presence within the intimate
> being of the soul. Consequently, the person desiring to
> find God must go forth from all created things according
> to affection and will, and enter within him/herself in
> deepest recollection . . . The Lord is hidden within the
> soul. It is there that the true contemplative must seek him
> with love [and in faith].[3]

In other words, God is so awesomely yet subtly present within
us that we can no longer encounter him as before.

Our insistence that the Lord come to us as he previously
did misdirects our quest on three accounts:

(a) We continue looking for the Lord everywhere except
where he is most intimately found. We are still searching for
him in sensory manifestations, in fond memories, in creatures
both within and outside ourselves. The Trinity is encountered
through dark faith deep within the most intimate being of the
soul. There God abides in transforming and purifying love.

(b) We insist on pursuing the Lord in a manner which can
never approach him in the fullness we crave. We persist in
seeking him by our own efforts, with our own initiative, out of
our own mental and emotional framework.

(c) We persist in seeking some-thing from God rather
than God in himself. We are still preoccupied with feeling
good about our prayer, with being consoled in our spiritual life,
with knowing precisely on which rung of the ladder of interior
progress we are situated. We are still trying to get some-thing
out of God, rather than humbly receiving God himself.

(3) *Everything*

What does the Mystical Doctor mean in the text cited
above by the expression "all created things" (*todas las cosas*)?
He means literally everything. Time and again John uses that
or an equivalent phrase to refer to absolutely every created

---

3. *Canticle*, 1, 6.

being: whether natural or "supernatural," whether in heaven or on earth, whether persons or inanimate things.[4]

In other words, "all created things" denotes every being that is not God himself, whether the creature is capable of being divinized, is an instrument of divinization or is already divinized. We "must go forth" from them all, including this earthly existence. There are no exceptions.

(4) We Must Go Forth from Everything

To "go forth from all created things according to affection and will" is a refrain in the vocabulary of St. John of the Cross.

John insists on going forth — *salir* — from all things rather than withdrawing — *separarse, apartarse, retirarse* — from anything. The accent falls on the positive movement toward God, in God, rather than away from some creature. Furthermore, there is not the slightest indication — either in John's life or in his writings — suggesting that the contemplative person (and there is a contemplative thrust in every human being!)[5] should or even can dispense with the normal and providential need of creatures in the process of interiorization. Nonetheless, because of the relationship of creature to Creator and because of the movement from scatteredness to transforming union, the way of authentic spiritualization demands an unqualified detachment of the will with respect to all that is not God himself. A careful balance is always necessary. It consists in the ability to make use of everything that comes from God in order to return to him without, however, stopping anywhere along the way.

The Mystical Doctor furnishes an apt example of the need and providential use of creatures in our life, on the one hand, together with complete detachment of the will with regard to them, on the other. Citing several biblical passages concerning detachment, John quotes the Latin Vulgate rendition of Luke 14:33.

---

4. For example: *ninguna cosa de la tierra ni del cielo (Canticle* 6, 7); *todas las cosas de arriba y de abajo (Night* I, 11, 1); *todas las cosas, así sensuales como espirituales (Ascent*, II, 1, 1); *naturales como sobrenaturales (Ascent*, III, 2, 3); *sin poder gustar de cosa ni divina ni humana (Night*, II, 16, 1).
5. See *Contemplation*, pp. 13-20; *Spiritual Direction*, pp. 15-32; *Spiritual Journey*, pp. 39-52, 89-95.

Qui non renúntiat ómnibus quae póssidet,
non pótest méus ésse discípulus.

Then John goes on to translate that logion of Jesus for his reader. Doing so, he carefully adds his own interpretation:

> Whoever does not give up *with his/her will* everything
> s/he possesses cannot be my disciple.[6]

The sense is this: What we must "give up" above all is not the creature as such, but our "will" regarding him, her or it. Clearly, there is no question of denying our power to love, to desire or to choose; or of negating our natural appetites, inclinations or preferences; or of destroying our ability to consent, to enjoy or to be happy. Rather, we give up our will as stopped, fixed or riveted on a creature by letting go the attachment.

Even though in a general sense all creatures are capable of assisting our quest for God, the actual presence or absence of a specific creature does not of itself directly help or impede that search. Whether that creature aids or obstructs depends on our inner disposition toward him, her or it. Thus, the will attaching itself to a creature which is present or coveting something or someone who is absent — in other words, stopping itself — cannot continue on to the Goal of its search who is God.

The object of detachment, therefore, is not the creature itself, but rather the *fixation of the will* on a creature. Thus, the crux of the problem is within us, not outside us. The person, situation or thing that we desire does not of itself hold us back from our movement in God. The issue is our attitude toward that creature. What impedes spiritual progress is not immersion in the world, but rather engrossment with the created.

At the beginning of *The Ascent* (I, 3, 1-4), John emphasizes that fact:

6. *Ascent*, I, 5, 2.

> We are not speaking here of the mere absence of crea-
> tures, since that of itself would not strip the soul of them
> as long as it still coveted them. Instead, we are talking
> about the detachment of the will . . . for creatures. Only
> in that way are we left free and empty of our attachments
> for them, even if we continue to possess and to enjoy
> them.

Every fixation disables the will. It invites impulsiveness:
"I want what I want simply because I want it." Compulsive
desire blocks out reason and common sense. The emotional
constellation surrounding the creature of our fascination im-
pairs and distorts our perception and judgment. The fixation of
our will thus severely limits our freedom and choices.

The intensity of a fixation upon a creature can range from
bare attachment to blatant addiction. Whatever the degree, the
arresting of our desire on the person or the thing obstructs our
passage-all-the-way-through creation to God in himself. For
God is God. S/he is not creation. Yet, the Lord abides within
the innermost being of each creature, while continuing to
transcend it entirely. Consequently, the person who would
encounter God must pass-all-the-way-through creation, not
circumvent it.

Nonetheless, when the will does become attached, addicted or codependent, that fixation can be turned to our favor.
Very often, the fixation of our will, because of its scope and
consequences, forces us to confront the true situation behind
our misguided wants and actions. Frequently, an addiction or
an attachment — once we recognize it — catapults us on a path
to healing which we would not otherwise have pursued. It is as
if the fixation is a symptom of an inner woundedness crying out
for redemption. The fixation of our will is like a warning signal
amplified to peak intensity, demanding that we deal with the
inner hurt or deprivation. Sometimes, we have to hit rock
bottom before we are able to admit our true need.

From that perspective, the arresting of the will on a
creature becomes in God's providence an inducement to heal-

ing and wholeness. The fixation becomes, in the long run, a formidable catalyst of divine transforming and purifying love. By a mysterious reversal, the fixation actually accelerates the pilgrim's forward movement on the spiritual journey. Its correction becomes a *blessed night.*

(5) *We Must Go Forth in Order to Enter*

As for the image of "going forth," John explains it in the following manner:

> This spiritual departure may be understood, first, as a going forth from all things through contempt and aversion for them; second, as a going out of oneself through forgetfulness of self. [7]

That statement of the Mystical Doctor is set in very negative if not forbidding terms. Taken literally, one must ask how Christian such an attitude really is. Furthermore, the image of going forth in this context is puzzling: If one must find God within oneself, would it not be more accurate to *enter into* self rather than to depart from self? That question does not escape John's attention, for earlier he stated that in order to perfect the union of love already established between the soul and the Lord "it is fitting for the soul . . . to enter within itself in deepest recollection," communing there with God in love. [8]

What then is meant by the analogy of a spiritual departure from all things and from oneself in order to enter more deeply within self for the sake of communing there with God?

It is this: The Lord is infinitely beyond yet intimately within each creature. The creature is *from* God and *to* God. It may also be capable of being divinized. Nonetheless, the creature is not God, nor does it contain him fully. The privileged place where we ultimately encounter the Lord is the intimate center of our being. There the Trinity dwells in love.

We make that discovery in two ways: one positive and the other negative — or at least that is how our senses interpret it.

7. *Canticle,* 1, 20.
8. *Canticle,* 1, 6.

Positively, the discovery comes about through contemplation; negatively, it happens through the gradual purification of the person with regard to everything created (self included). The concentration of that *purifying contemplation* is upon the human will in such a way that God communicating himself to us in love consumes every trace of egocentrism and removes every attachment. Thus God abiding within our deepest self eventually breaks the impasse of selfishness, regardless of its form or manifestation. We are liberated from selfishness and scatteredness not to shun our gifts, but rather with them to pass on to deeper union with God and creation.

B. Letting Go Defense Mechanisms

From a practical point of view, a difficult aspect of this going forth is getting past the defense mechanisms which we have consciously or unconsciously built up over the years. Those defenses are formidable obstacles to progress in God. Perhaps that is the reason John attacks them with such vehemence: "through contempt and aversion for creatures . . . through forgetfulness of self."

Those coping strategies block us, stop us and constrain us. They barricade us behind invincible walls where we refuse to let anyone in, including God. They keep us on guard, fighting to maintain our present ground instead of progressing. If we are to move forward on our spiritual journey, those indomitable fortifications have to come down. We have to let go the coping mechanisms which we use to cover up our pain and to ward off further hurt.

The need to let go defenses marks a point of convergence between recovery from addiction, codependency and attachments and the quest for God described by John of the Cross in stanza 1 of *The Spiritual Canticle*. Recovery is actually a dimension of the mystery of God's seeking out of the person and of the individual's quest for God in response. In recovery, we become free of our false self as we reclaim and develop our true identity. Yet, in discovering our true identity, we discover

God indwelling us. We encounter ourselves at that depth where:

> I live now, no longer I,
> but Christ lives in me (Gal 2:20).

Some people may have been consciously fostering an intimate relationship with God prior to the recognition of their addiction, codependency or attachments. Recovery in their case coincides with a new threshold in their already deliberate quest for the Lord. For others, however, the beginning of recovery and the moment when they become aware of their search for God occur simultaneously.

As we let go our defense mechanisms, we experience a feeling of growing vulnerability. That vulnerability is a necessary condition for communion with self, creation and God. It means having a heart of flesh instead of a heart of stone (Ezk 36:26). It means standing open to the influences of God within events, encounters and relationships. It means sharing ourselves with others, sometimes even at the risk of being hurt. It means being in touch with our feelings, perceptions, thoughts, desires and needs. Vulnerability requires willingness to suffer the tension between our desire for intimacy and our tendency toward withdrawal. In that vulnerability, the recovering person receives support from creatures, yet continues to pass on to God through them.

The thrust of our quest for God is toward increasing intimacy with self, others, creation and the indwelling Trinity. Those relationships form the matrix of recovery from addictions, codependency and attachments. Paradoxically, that intimacy opens recovering persons to the painful but salvific experience of the Lord's seeming absence. Letting go our defense mechanisms and letting God heal us his way opens us to receive God's wound of love.

Having studied stanza 1 of *The Spiritual Canticle*, let us proceed to develop more specifically the positive contribution of creatures in the process of purification: stanzas 2 to 7.

CHAPTER 7

THE POSITIVE YET PURIFYING ROLE OF CREATURES IN GREATER DETAIL

Several times in his writings, St. John of the Cross uses this literary device: He opens abruptly with a startling statement which rivets the attention of his readers. Then, in order to establish the context in which his initial assertions can be more accurately understood, he proceeds with an ample explanation. The positive yet purifying role of creation in our transformation as presented in *The Spiritual Canticle* is an application of that methodology. Thus, John begins abruptly:

> Where have you hidden yourself,
> O my Beloved, having left me in anguish?
> You fled like the deer,
> Having wounded me.
> I went forth searching frantically for you, and you were gone.

In that opening stanza, John describes in just twenty-two Spanish words of masterful poetry one of the most complex issues of the spiritual journey. That is, the apparent absence of God by reason of the intensification of his presence within us. That experience, so concisely expressed by the Mystical Doctor, caps a long history of divine preparation within each person. Moreover, the experience is situated within a broader mystical and theological context.

Having captured his reader's attention, John proceeds to fill in that context.

A. *Spiritual Canticle: Stanzas 2-7 in General*

Throughout stanzas 2-7, John treats specifically of the knowledge (*el conocimiento*) of creatures. He addresses successively: self-knowledge, knowledge of nonpersonal creation and knowledge of persons.

In this context, the meaning that the Mystical Doctor gives the term "knowledge" approaches more the biblical usage of the word than the scholastic. Thus he stresses the experiential dimension of knowledge, together with the ability to reflect sagaciously on that experience. In these stanzas, John accentuates the providential need for direct personal involvement with creation. He emphasizes the mature and intentional use of creatures in the process of divinization. Furthermore, in the case of knowledge of persons (stanza 7), he refers specifically to the need for meaningful interpersonal relationships.

B. *Self-Knowledge and Detachment: Stanzas 2-3*

John of the Cross's first step in constructing the broader theological context of stanza 1 consists in what is generally called the beginning of adult spiritual life (stanzas 2-3). This is the threshold and the stage of "Immersion in Creation for Christ" where critical self-knowledge leads to active purification and meditative prayer. [1]

Undoubtedly, the single most important creature in the life of each of us is our self — our unique personhood, our singular individuality. It is within that matrix that all transformation and purgation occur. There, the Trinity abides in love.

The basic principle underlying John's theology of self-knowledge and active purification is this:

---

1. See *Spiritual Journey*, pp. 51-95.

The more we come to experience our true self and God in us, the better we perceive the fixations of our will upon certain creatures.

What do we do then? How do we deal with the fixation and get moving again? We strip our will with respect to the creature in question. That is, we take positive action to remove the fixation, but not necessarily the creature.

The term which John uses in this connection is very graphic — *desnudar/desnudez*. The active verb means: to strip, to undress, to uncover. The reflexive verb signifies: to take off one's clothes, to deprive oneself of, to rid oneself of. The noun expresses nudity, nakedness. The prime object of all this stripping, however, is the fixation of the will on some creature, rather than the creature itself. The creature as such must be let go, without necessarily being discarded.

In the history of spirituality, a variety of English words have been used to render what John calls "stripping." Several of them have been grossly misunderstood: mortify/mortification, deny/denial, renounce/renunciation, abnegate/abnegation. Literally, to mortify one's will can mean to kill it — to render oneself impassive, emotionless, apathetic. Strictly speaking, to deny oneself can mean to work deliberately at the destruction of one of our greatest gifts — our self, our personhood, our individuality. Understood without proper nuance, to renounce or to abnegate one's desires could mean to reject, to nullify, to prohibit their presence or their message.

To interpret the above classical terminology in that vein is not only counterproductive spiritually, but also potentially disastrous emotionally and mentally. Yet, the above words have biblical roots. For example: the idea of mortification comes from Colossians 3:5:

> Put to death — *nekrósate* — whatever belongs to your earthy nature: evil desires, covetousness, etc.

The notions of self-denial, renunciation and abnegation are derived from Mark 8:34-35 and parallels:

If anyone wishes to come after me,
     let him/her deny self — *aparnesástho eautón* —
     and take up his/her cross . . .

Those terms can, therefore, have a valid meaning. Thus the immediate object of mortification is not strictly my will or the creature in my life but the fixation of my will on that creature. The proper object of self-denial is not exactly my self, but my selfishness. The appropriate object of renunciation and abnegation is neither my desire nor my passion, but my engrossment in some person, situation or thing. Thus I do not kill my emotions or disregard the creatures which God puts on my path. I rather address the crux of the problem which is my refusing to move on through creation.

There is yet another English word which renders the *desnudez* of John of the Cross: "detachment." That is a more felicitous term than mortification, self-denial, renunciation or abnegation. The image which it conjures up expresses more directly the basic analogy of breaking the fixation. To detach oneself means to untie that which holds one bound so as to be able to get moving again. Detachment is used in contradistinction to attachment, which in this context means to allow one's forward progress to come to a halt. Addiction and codependency are the extreme forms of attachment. Detachment, therefore, is integral to every recovery process.

In stanzas 2-3 of *The Spiritual Canticle,* John addresses what has come to be called "active" detachment. That is, as a positive response to some insight about myself, I do something constructive to counteract my fixation on a creature. For example: I now realize that when I am in a bad mood I tend to pig out on ice cream. So instead of guzzling down half a gallon, I limit myself to one or two scoops. Or, perhaps in lieu of eating anything at all, I listen to uplifting music or talk about my moodiness with a friend. Whichever method of detachment I choose, it affects my involvement with the creature in such a way that I respond more maturely — that is, less attached — than I did before having arrived at that self-knowledge.

Most detachments come about by undergoing in faith and love the diminishments which occur in the course of living: restrictions of diet, inclemency of weather, bereavements, the aging process, etc. At God's prompting, detachment may also be accomplished by voluntarily sacrificing, by drastically cutting down or by abstaining altogether from certain goods which cause pleasure. Ultimately, however, *desnudez* is effected by allowing ourselves to be penetrated "passively" by the purifying action of God in contemplation. That form of detachment is unmistakably the most efficacious. Yet each of the others remains relatively necessary throughout life.

It can be difficult to discern whether a specific affection is in reality a loving search for God in and through creation or a fixation of the will. In actual fact, there is always a certain mingling of those two elements every step along the way. Hence, there must be as much detachment regarding a particular creature as there is will to love her, him or it. Moreover, authentic discernment as to exactly what requires detaching and in what measure remains extremely delicate. Therefore, lest we cut off something vital, we very quickly find ourselves obliged to let ourselves be purified passively by God (Jn 15:1-2). For we can never completely sort out the intricacies of all our wills and desires, of all our pleasures and enjoyments, of all our affections and gratifications. God's pruning, stripping, purging will be infinitely more effective than anything we ourselves could ever accomplish or imagine.

Detachment must attain not only the will, but every facet of the human person. All desires, pleasures and enjoyments undergo intense purification. Eventually, every attachment must be detached.

To strip our will and to detach our desire mean, therefore, to be led by a desire for God so intense that we cannot stop until we rest entirely in him.

C. *Passing Through Creatures, Not Around Them: Stanzas 4-5*

Even though detachment arises from a positive need and
awareness within the person, s/he nonetheless experiences it
as something painful. In the context of the maturing soul, the
most obvious source of that pain is the realization that nothing
created can bring back the Beloved as before. This is so
because God is now calling the person forward into ever deeper
mystery. In that state of mind, the searching soul addresses
creation:

> O forests and thickets,
> Planted by the hand of my Beloved,
> O meadows of green
> Adorned with flowers,
> Tell me, has he passed through [*por*] you? (Stanza 4)

Some translators render the *por* in the Spanish text as
"by" rather than "through." Though grammatically possible,
"by" can be theologically misleading. John is stressing that the
Word entered and passed *through* creation in virtue of his
incarnation, death and resurrection. Jesus did not go around
it, over it or under it. He did not pass it up or pass it by.
Therefore, the true follower of Christ must do likewise. On the
spiritual journey, s/he too has to pass-all-the-way-through
creation, not circumvent it.

In response, creation recognizes the gifts it has received
from its Creator as well as their place in his plan:

> Pouring out a thousand graces,
> He passed through [*por*] these groves in haste.
> And beholding them as he went,
> With his glance alone
> Left them all clothed in beauty (Stanza 5).

Yes indeed, he passed through creation "in haste"; that is,
without stopping, without getting hung up, without becoming
attached to anyone or anything anywhere along the way.

D. The Wound of Mature Love: Stanza 6

In the next stanza, John of the Cross elaborates in some detail his understanding of the role of creation in divinization. He introduces his remarks in this manner:

> In the living contemplation and knowledge of creatures, the soul beholds the immense fullness of graces, virtue and beauty with which God has gifted them.[2]

That observation is not particular to the Mystical Doctor. Any person of good will would perceive as much. However, building upon that basis, John offers a deeper insight. At a certain threshold in the process of spiritualization, God dwelling and operating from deep within our innermost being intensifies his transforming activity to the point of thrusting us more profoundly into the obscure way of the night. The role of creatures — without changing direction — becomes more acutely purifying.

> [Thus] the soul — wounded in love by this trace of the beauty of its Beloved, a beauty that it has experienced in creatures, and anxious to see God's invisible beauty — speaks the following verses:

> Who has the power to heal me?
> Cease surrendering yourself to me in this manner.
> Do not send me
> Any other messengers,
> Since they cannot give me what I yearn for.[3]

The truth underlying that stanza may be summarized this way: Because God is immanent in every creature, the more we experience creation in its depths, the more we know *of* or *about* its Creator. An increase in knowledge of God through creatures causes an intensification of love for him. That love in turn

2. *Canticle*, 6, 1.
3. *Ibid.*

increases our yearning to encounter the Beloved in himself so as to enjoy complete union with him.

Yet there is more to this mystery. The deeper experience of God through creation not only brings about an increase in love, but also it effects an increase in suffering.

Why? How? In becoming more conscious of God, we see all the more clearly that no creature, however excellent, is the One whom we relentlessly seek. Only the Beloved can fulfill in perfect and consummated love the inexhaustible yearnings of the human heart. In this way, we are wounded ever more painfully by our thirst to be possessed completely by God, on the one hand and, on the other, by the inability of any creature to give him in the plenitude we crave. That wound of love hollows out a painful vacuum within us which only God himself can fill.

The more we are drawn into transforming union in this life, the more deeply we experience the wound of love. John of the Cross speaks of three successive phases of wounding in relation to ever intensifying spiritualization:

> *herida* — a surface wound (*Canticle*, 1);
> *llaga* — a deeper, more inflamed wound (*Canticle*, 7);
> *cauterio* — wound by fire, cauterization (*Flame*, 2).

In other contexts, John treats amply of the wounds we inflict on ourselves by sinfulness, selfishness and self-indulgence. Those are wounds of *false love* — the woundedness causing or ensuing from our addictions, codependency and attachments.

In the present context, however, John accentuates the wound inflicted by the *mature love* of God through creatures. In essence, that wound is the realization that we cannot be completely satisfied by anyone or anything except God in himself. Thus, the term "wound of love" does not refer to the dissatisfaction or the negative attitudes which result from painful experiences. It expresses rather the normal and providential consequence of authentic Christian involvement; that is, the inability of creatures to satiate completely the infinite longing of the human heart.

Thus, fully conscious of having been wounded by love, the soul cries out:

> "Who can heal me?" Which means: Of all the gratifications of the world, all the pleasures of the senses, all the delights of the spirit, not a single one is able to heal me, nothing can satiate me . . . Not only that . . . but they increase my craving to see my Beloved as he is in himself. In this way, the glimpses of God which I experience from knowledge, feeling or any other communication are like messengers who teach me something about him. They quicken and excite my appetite all the more, as do crumbs in an intense hunger.[4]

The Sanjuanist theology of the cross inherent in that perception of creation is profoundly positive. True Christian appreciation of creatures causes an emptiness, an experience of absence which only God can fill. In this manner, the creature as creature perfectly accomplishes its purpose. It demonstrates experientially that it is from God and to God without ever becoming a god. Furthermore, in-depth knowledge of and mature affection for creation are not only tolerable but also providentially necessary. They enable us to experience even more acutely the positive void within ourselves which that very knowledge and love produce.

In spiritual direction, it is often difficult to determine the source of a person's feelings of unfulfillment, emptiness, longing, restlessness, etc. Are they arising primarily from the wound of love, or principally from the person's craving for fulfillment of unmet developmental needs? Are the feelings resulting from an at-homeness in God which incites yearning for more of God, or do they originate in a directee's insecurity and low self-esteem?

Both the director and the directee need to address the possible influence of denied or repressed abandonment.

---

4. *Canticle*, 6, 3-4.

Should the directee be already aware of the existence of such issues, s/he and the director have to discern how to best minimize their effects.

Those questions are important in discerning a possible call to increased solitude in one's daily life regardless of lifestyle. Yet they become especially crucial when examining a possible vocation to the contemplative or the eremitical life. For, when the wound of abandonment is the driving force, then what the person calls "God" and "solitude" may in fact be no more than an object of attachment or even an addiction.

Once God has brought us through the threshold of spiritual adulthood,[5] however, s/he takes possession of us even more directly, yet always in a manner which enhances our individual freedom. The Lord accomplishes that transition progressively with our active participation. Thus, to the degree that we seek him, God himself quickens and directs our search by the loving wound of his absence — a wound which is produced by his transcendent immanence.

From a certain point of view, the experience which we call a feeling of God's absence is an illusion. In reality, the Lord is more present and more directly operative within us than ever before. Nevertheless, from another point of view, that sense of distance is very real. God, for all his love and intimacy, remains wholly Other. Each encounter with him in faith through creatures intensifies that realization. Thus, deeper awareness of the immanence of the Beloved serves only to increase our appreciation of his utter transcendence, for the immanence of God always remains transcendent.

Having enabled us to taste the splendors of creation, God then causes us to experience unmistakably through that encounter our inexhaustible yearning to abandon ourselves unreservedly to him, our Creator and Beloved. In that respect, the images of abyss, hunger, and thirst serve to accentuate the consciousness of our limitless receptivity to the Lord. Only the person who is fixated on some creature is engulfed or imprisoned. The soul who proceeds on its way toward God through

5. See *Spiritual Journey*, pp. 13-15, 39-52, 55-95.

creation reaches its Goal. Its heart is becoming ever more opened to the One-Thing-Necessary (Lk 10:42). Thus creatures fulfill their mission:

> The finite has opened our heart to the Infinite.
> The created has made us more receptive to the
> Uncreated.

The Mystical Doctor summarizes those truths in the following prayer:

> Lord, my Spouse, what you gave of yourself to me in part, give now entirely. What you show in glimpses, show now in full light . . . communicating yourself by yourself. It seems at times in your visits that you are going to give me the jewel of possessing you. Then, when I examine myself more carefully, I find that I am deprived of you in the way I crave to have you . . . Therefore, surrender yourself, now giving yourself completely to all my being so that I may possess you totally. Henceforth, cease sending me messengers who do not know how to tell me what I seek . . . Nothing in heaven or on earth can give me the experience I so pine to have of you . . . Instead of those messengers, O Lord, may you yourself be both the Messenger and the Message.[6]

E. *Interpersonal Relationships: Stanza 7*

The seventh stanza of *The Spiritual Canticle* both concludes St. John of the Cross's presentation on the positive role of creatures in our sanctification and, at the same time, introduces a deeper phase of the wound of love. In stanzas 4-6, John referred principally to nonpersonal creation — what we would call "things." Now, in stanza 7, he treats specifically of involvement with persons other than oneself.

Endowed with intelligence, free will and immortality,

6. *Canticle*, 6, 6-7.

human beings are the crown of creation. Mature love for another person, therefore, carries with it much greater potential for experience of God. This, in turn, causes such an increase in the wound of love that John even changes the word *herida* (in stanzas 1-6) to *llaga* (in stanza 7).

Thus, in the theology of the Mystical Doctor not only are nature and some synthetic goods necessary in the process of our gradual transformation in God, but persons together with interpersonal involvements and commitments constitute an even more crucial catalyst in opening us to uncreated grace. Creatures, especially people, are essential to the actualization of our receptivity to God.

Essential to the recovery process of addicted, codependent and attached persons are intimate relationships. And, essential to those relationships is acceptance of an increase in the wound of love. Before recovery, those people had tried desperately to avoid pain. Now, in recovery they face an even more intense wounding. But this time, they allow it to open them to deeper joy.

How is that possible? John explains:

> Even though this *blessed night* darkens the spirit,
>   it does so only to impart light in all things.
> And even though it humbles us and reveals our miseries,
>   it does so only to exalt us.
> And even though it impoverishes us and empties us of all
>   our possessions and natural affections,
>   it does so only that we may stretch forward divinely
>   in our enjoyment of everything in heaven and on earth,
>   while preserving a general freedom of spirit in them all.[7]

---

7. *Night*, II, 9, 1.

CHAPTER 8

PURIFICATION AS
INTEGRAL TO UNION WITH GOD

When we speak of St. John of the Cross and purification, our
thoughts turn spontaneously to the dark night. That phrase
refers to his eight-stanza poem, *En una noche oscura*, probably
written within a few days of his prison break in 1578. The
phrase evokes also the two commentaries he began on that
poem, but never completed: *The Ascent of Mount Carmel* (c.
1582) and *The Dark Night of the Soul* (c. 1585). The phrase
denotes, furthermore, a teaching which occupies a central
place in all his works.

A. *The Dark Night of the Soul*

The expression "dark night" is the prime analogy which
John uses to describe the purgative side of transformation.
Both transformation and the dark night of the soul begin for
each of us at the moment of individual creation and endure
until personal death/resurrection. God's transforming love and
purifying activity affect every aspect of our mortal existence.
Our whole earthly sojourn moves forward within those two
all-embracing and interacting influences.

St. Paul expresses that mystery in the dialectic of the
aging and maturing process:

> Although exteriorly we are falling into decay
>   [i.e., passing through the night],
>   interiorly we are being renewed day by day
>   [i.e., being transformed in God by God] (2 Cor 4:16).[1]

Or, as John the Baptizer expresses basically the same truth:

> I must decrease
>   so that he [Christ] may increase (Jn 3:30).

Night and transformation, falling into decay and being renewed day by day, decreasing and increasing converge upon our personal death/resurrection. At that threshold, when our humanity is most weak and mortal, the transforming activity of God within us is most powerful (1 Cor 15:54-57; 2 Cor 12:10; 13:4). The process of purification and transformation, however, is painful from beginning to end. Yet, paradoxically, that very pain remains a basic fact of living and of learning to live more joyfully.

Addicted, codependent and attached persons try at virtually any cost to avoid pain, while unwittingly inflicting indescribable misery on both themselves and others. Recovery from addiction, codependency and attachment, therefore, requires that we face squarely the hurt inherent in living and in learning to live more fully. Recovery invites us to pass through the dark night. Thus, in faith we transverse suffering and death to encounter God abiding in our inmost being.

Each word in the phrase "*dark night* of the *soul*"[2] has special connotations in the framework of the Mystical Doctor.

"*Dark*" is an analogy for painful. Philosophers would call it "evil." It is what hurts regardless of its source. In the Hebrew Scriptures, dark (*hoshék*) frequently denotes calamity and misery. "An intense and dreadful darkness came over" Abram as God revealed to him the future slavery and degradation of his descendants in Egypt (Gn 15:12-13).

---

1. See *Spiritual Journey*, pp. 19-32, 39-52 (esp. 41).
2. *Ibid.*, pp. 99-113.

The dark aspect of the night accentuates all the forms of adversity which we undergo in the course of living and being transformed. Much of that adversity arises out of our own inner poverty, from emotional weaknesses, psychological limitations, personal sinfulness, addictions, codependency, attachments, etc. It assails us also from the outside: disease, harsh words, unjust accusations, etc. God integrates all that pain into our night, cooperating with us to convert into good our passage through those diminishments.

"*Night,*" on the other hand, is an analogy for mystery. In the Hebrew Scriptures, night (*layíl*) sometimes connotes distress and anxiety. Frequently, however, it is symbolic of the mysterious activity of God within us and all around us. It was, for example, at night that Jacob encountered Yahweh face to face (Gn 32:22-30). It is also in the course of the night that the Lord probes our heart and examines our inmost being (Ps 17:3). Creation not only proclaims the glory of God during the day, but also "night after night displays knowledge of him" (Ps 19:2).

The New Testament perpetuates the same symbolic usage of and distinction between darkness (*skótos*) and night (*nux*) as do the Hebrew Scriptures. *Skótos,* especially when employed in conjunction with the symbolism of the demonic, frequently denotes moral and spiritual misery. Night, on the other hand, often evokes the mysterious working of God. "It was night" when Judas departed and Jesus began his final discourse (Jn 13:30). The Lord comes unannounced — not only at the parousia, but also at significant moments during our lives — "like a thief in the night" (1 Th 5:2; 2 P 3:10). Nicodemus sought out Jesus "by night" not only because it was safer, but also to imbibe his mystery (Jn 3:2; 19:39).

"*Soul.*" The Mystical Doctor employs the word in a sense that transcends the classical scholastic usage. He uses it with the traditional mystical meaning derived from the Hebrew *nephésh* and the New Testament *psyché.* "Soul" thus denotes the whole person being acted upon by God, but stressing the interior dimensions of personhood.

Thus, the *dark night* of the *soul* is truly very painful. But far more importantly, it is mysteriously salvific. We reel from the suffering it causes, even as we are being filled with the hope that it promises. On a first-impression conscious level, it seems that we experience more darkness than night. In a more mature and reflective disposition, however, we realize that there is infinitely more mystery than pain:

> I believe that what we suffer in this life cannot begin to
> compare with the glory which is awaiting us (Rm 8:18).

Our darkness is the mysteriously consuming and purgative side of transformation. For the same flame of divine love unites us to God and purges all that is un-Godlike in us. It is because we are being so completely transformed that we are being so intensely purified — like gold in a furnace (Pr 17:3; 1 P 1:6-7).

That fire of divine love causes in us an overwhelming experience of inner poverty. From the deepest recesses of our being, that flame drives up into consciousness the awareness of our woundedness, weakness and sinfulness. Hitherto we had successfully kept them hidden behind defense mechanisms. As God's light pierces those survival strategies and we let them go, we have to face our limitations as never before. We have the impression that we are worse than ever: more lustful, irascible, resentful, selfish. The truth of the matter is, however, that we have always been that way, only we could not bring ourselves to admit it. Now that we can no longer hide from our inner poverty, we are much better off spiritually.

In the midst of all the pain, anxiety and darkness, we realize that God's love is not punitive. It is always medicinal, geared toward correction and growth (Pr 3:11-12; Heb 12:5-13; Jm 1:2-4, 12). Whatever affliction we suffer is not caused directly by God. It springs from our woundedness, our self-centeredness and our weaknesses as they come face to face with the transformative activity of God within us.

We would not experience the fire of divine love as oppressive if it had not so much to purge. Once we are sufficiently purified, however, our focus on the darkness of the night shifts to a profound appreciation of and delight in the blessings of the night.

St. John of the Cross distinguishes several stages of darkness: the night of sense, the night of spirit, the tranquil night, the serene night.[3] Since the first two encompass the greater part of people's lives, we resume John's description of them.[4]

B. *The Night of Sense in Relation to the Night of Spirit*

"Senses" is a term which John of the Cross uses to indicate the more observable aspects of the human person. John speaks consistently of the "senses of the soul" rather than "of the body."[5]

The Mystical Doctor distinguishes the *senses* of the soul from the *spiritual part* of the soul. That is, he differentiates our behavioral aspects from our mysterious depths. Thus, the dark night of the soul can be viewed basically from two viewpoints: the night of sense and the night of spirit — the second being a more radical intensification of the first.

The senses of the soul, therefore, are more than sight, hearing, touch, taste and smell. They comprise also our emotions, imagination, memory, mind and will. Although some of the latter perform spiritual and qualitative functions (such as reflection, understanding, loving), they nevertheless pertain to the sensory (or observable) aspect of the person.

The night of sense is that aspect of purgation which corresponds to God's loving transformation of us at the threshold and stage of emergence through creation with Christ.[6] It describes the kenotic (Ph 3:7) element of beginning

---

3. *Ibid.*, p. 39-52.
4. Regarding the tranquil night and the serene night, see *Spiritual Journey*, pp. 209-211 and 216-219.
5. See e.g.: *Ascent*, I, 1, 2; *Night*, II, 3; *Contemplation*, pp. 44-52.
6. See *Spiritual Journey*, pp. 41, 97-131.

to surrender to Father, Son and Spirit the self we have laboriously developed over the course of life. The immediate cause of the night is transforming union. The principal cause of its darkness — that is, of the pain — is our immaturity, our resistance, our woundedness, our inner poverty.

The night of sense and the night of spirit are in reality one night of the soul in successive stages. They can be compared to the difference between sundown and midnight, between pruning a branch and pulling up a root, between washing out a fresh stain and scrubbing out an old deeply embedded one.[7] The night of sense is more accurately a curbing and a bridling of our passions rather than a radical purgation of them. This is so because all our behavioral patterns, attachments and immature dependencies are rooted within the unconscious. Therefore:

> Until the spirit is sufficiently purged, the sensate dimension of the human person cannot be thoroughly purified. In the night of spirit, then, both our sensate and spiritual aspects are purged together, since one is never truly purified without the other.[8]

The phrase "night of spirit" thus denotes a radical transformation and purification of our whole being. That purgation directly penetrates both our behavior and our most spiritual core.

C. General Characteristics of the Night

The first stanza of John of the Cross's celebrated poem on the subject begins with these impassioned words:

> In a dark night,
> Enflamed with love's urgent longings,
> — O happy chance! —
> I went forth unnoticed;
> My house being already at rest.

7. See *Night*, II, 2, 1; *Spiritual Journey*, pp. 163-172.
8. See *Night*, II, 3, 1.

In those verses, the Mystical Doctor describes the fundamental breakthrough which results as God takes definitive possession of each person. Thus John presents in moving imagery several essential characteristics of purification: It is a down-to-earth part of our life history. It is received in/by us. It propels us forward. It establishes us in peace.

(1) *We Experience the Dark Night as True-to-Life.*

In order to appreciate the fact that John is recounting in the above stanza not only a personal mystical threshold, but also a very specific historical event — namely, his nocturnal escape from prison — it suffices to stroll along *El Paseo del Carmen* in Toledo, Spain. There one can stand on the approximate spot where John, emaciated from dysentery and nine months of solitary confinement, jumped to freedom on a moonless August night in 1578. One need only peer at the jagged cliff which rose up from the raging Tajo River at the foot of the ancient wall of Carmel to imagine some of the unspeakable terror and relief that must have filled his heart as he jumped from a second story balcony to the narrow ridge of wall below. Had he missed the top of the wall to the inside, he would have broken on a stone patio every bone in his enfeebled body. Had he missed the top of the wall to the outside, he would have been swept away in the swift current. John had to land just right, in total darkness. He did, with ingenuity, luck and God's grace.

Purgation is always radically down-to-earth. It permeates not only the crises events of our lives, but also the most banal details of our daily existence. The specific form that purification takes at any moment is tailored by God to all the particulars, no matter how seemingly trivial or insignificant, of each human journey. As the concrete circumstances of our daily life change, so too the shape of our purification. No one escapes the consuming fire of divine love. For example: Spouses experience it in bearing with each other's idiosyncrasies. Parents struggle through it as they let their children grow up and become emancipated. Taxi drivers suffer it while fighting traffic and putting up with the insults of fares. We all pass through the dark night, for in virtue of the universal call to holiness everyone is called to transforming union.

(2) *We Undergo It.*

A second dimension essential to purification is that we undergo the night. Every truly salvific action within us is received. We do not save ourselves or one another. We *are saved* by God.

John emphasizes that point in a comment regarding the fourth line of the stanza in question:

> The soul goes forth — God wrenching it out —
>   solely because of his love. [9]

Our interior situation is described in that sentence by an active verb: "the soul goes forth." Immediately, however, John adds with insistence: "God wrenching it out." That is, this departure is in reality more an action of God than of the soul. The going forth is more received in us than performed by us, since it is the Lord who causes us to go forth. He breaks our shackles so that we can move freely out of our attachments, addictions and codependency more deeply into him.

The phrase "O happy chance" is another indication that we undergo the night. This going forth, this tearing out by the roots happens to us in the ordinary course of living. Moreover, we are indeed fortunate that it does occur!

Some translators render that phrase "O blessed grace." Yet John wrote *ventura* (chance), not *gracia* (grace). The nuance regarding divine activity and the dark night which the Mystical Doctor seems to make is that God does not so much cause the night as cooperate with us during our night. Pain, suffering, detachment, death happen in the course of living. They are not of themselves imposed on us by God. The Lord does not specifically ordain, for instance, that a person die of

---

9. *Ascent*, I, 1, 4. "— *Sacándola Dios* —": *sacar* means to extricate, to force out with determination, to rip out.

lung cancer. Perhaps s/he smoked too much or worked too long under unhealthy conditions, contracting the cancer as a result of a combination of circumstances. Yet God works with the person from within him/her to transform that illness into a salvific experience (1 Cor 1:18). One would not say that the cancer is God's will. The cancer remains unfortunate. What is, however, fortunate is that God wills to transform that aspect of the person's dark night into a grace — a *blessed night.*[10]

There certainly do exist what are termed "active purifications." These are the voluntary detachments which we undertake as a result of self-knowledge. For example, I realize that I push myself too hard. Therefore, I need to let go some of that intensity and re-channel my energy into more qualitative leisure. Yet, at best, those active purifications attain only the surface of our struggle to overcome attachments, addictions or codependency. God himself must directly prune us in our depths (Jn 15:1-2). Moreover, that deeper purification happens not as a punishment, but in love: "solely because of his love."[11]

(3) *It Moves Us Forward.*

A third characteristic of the dark night is its underlying movement, its relentless tension toward something better. The rhythm of the Spanish poetry reveals an energetic advance. The verb *salir* (to go forth) indicates both the act of leaving and the motion of leaping forward. God, having extricated us from our enmeshment, propels us forward. We are freed from attachments, addictions and codependency in order to proceed more directly on the way of Spirit.

(4) *We Experience Peace in Its Midst.*

A fourth characteristic of this night is its joyful peacefulness — but, a peace and a joy which the world can neither

---

10. See *Spiritual Journey*, pp. 21-32; *Called by God*, I, pp. 17-40.
11. *Solo por amor de él (Ascent*, I, 1, 4). John intends both senses of *de él*: God's love for us and our love for him.

comprehend nor give (Jn 14:27; 16:20-24). Peace exists in the midst of and despite the intensity of the purification. John stresses that truth in the second and fifth lines of the stanza in question.

In the second line, he juxtaposes love and urgent longing — literally: "with anguishes in loves enflamed." Fear, confusion, pain become very acute during some phases of the night. Yet, all the while, our innermost being burns with love. Even in the fiercest throes of the night of spirit, nothing can dull the conviction that God is really in control and will faithfully bring the turmoil to a joyful and peaceful resolution. In the fifth line of the stanza, John states the characteristic of peace even more directly: "my house [i.e., my inner self] being already at rest [i.e., in peace]."

Moreover, peace occurs during, on, in the course of the dark night itself — not only once it has passed. There will undoubtedly be a profound relief after we have completed our journey through the night. That completion, however, will come only in the resurrection. Since John is addressing this mortal existence, he stresses that now in the midst of the perplexities of our current purifications a very deep peace already exists.

That peace does not result from satisfaction of our desires or in relaxation from tension. Rather, it is the fruit of the purifying and transforming presence of God within us. Love, faith and hope intensify in proportion to the acuteness of the night. Suffering of itself is incapable of causing an increase of divine presence within us, yet total darkness is the necessary condition for complete abandonment to God. Rather than plunging us into sheer nothingness, however, the night is a "happy chance" — a veritable grace, a blessed event. As such, it becomes the most conducive milieu to facilitate the divinizing and pacifying activity of God within us. Not only can the world not bestow this peace, the world finds it impossible even to make any sense of it (1 Cor 1:22-25).

CHAPTER 9

THE DARK NIGHT AS AN INFLUENCE
OF GOD WITHIN THE SOUL

Recovery from addiction, codependency or attachment requires that we submit consciously to a transforming and purifying process. In so doing, we entrust ourselves to God's loving care, ready to let the Lord effect in us a spiritual awakening. Thus, we are thrust headlong into the dark night of the soul.

St. John of the Cross describes the night in various ways and approaches it from many angles. The following is one of his most succinct yet profound descriptions:

> The dark night is an influence of God within the soul [*una influencia de Dios en el alma*] which purges it of every kind of immaturity . . . That divine activity is none other than contemplation . . . By it God secretly instructs the soul in the perfection of love, without its doing anything or understanding how the Lord is operating. Inasmuch as this . . . contemplation is the loving wisdom of God, it causes two striking effects within the soul: purgation and illumination. In that way, it disposes the soul for union in love with God.[1]

In the mystical theology of John, God is clearly the one who produces the night — the principal agent, as it were.

1. *Night*, II, 5, 1.

Divinization, or transformation in God,[2] is the purpose of the
night — the goal, so to speak. The human person in all his/her
weaknesses and potentialities is that which is transformed —
the matter which is spiritualized.

What then makes the night night? It is the transforming
influence of God within us purifying us. God completely
permeates the human person. His loving activity gradually
purges every vestige of addiction, codependency and attachment. We cooperate most fully with that process of recovery by
receiving God and by letting him transform us.

John uses interchangeably the analogies of "purge/
purgation" and "purify/purification." Both notions are bibli-
cally based:

> If a person be purged of what is ignoble,
>   s/he can be an instrument for noble purposes (2 Tm 2:21).
> Draw near to God . . .
>   and let your hearts be purified (Jm 4:8).

Nevertheless, the Mystical Doctor retains a certain par-
tiality for the down-to-earthness of taking a purge — as in an
old-fashioned enema. The image of flushing out excrement is
not dainty. It may even shock the sensibilities of some people.
Yet John was never one to shy away from raw figurative
language.

A. Purgative Influence Within the Soul

Let us examine more closely the notion of God as a
purgative influence from within our inmost being.

To influence ordinarily means to act upon. So, if one must
use a preposition to express grammatically that fact, one
should normally use "upon" — *sobre*, in Spanish. One exerts
influence *upon* another. Notwithstanding, John of the Cross

---

2. See *Contemplation*, pp. 13-20; *Spiritual Direction*, pp. 15-32; *Spiritual Journey*, pp.
    19-21.

chooses the preposition *en* to accentuate the interiority of the source of this purgation. This is a purifying influence of God dwelling deep *within* the human person — rather than of God up there exerting some purgative influence on us down here.

How does John envisage that activity? In explaining the signs for discerning the authenticity of the night of sense, he specifically addresses the question. The first sign is the experience of finding neither satisfaction nor consolation in the things of God or in anything else created. While explicating that sign, the Mystical Doctor ascribes the aridity to this fact: God puts us in the dark night in order to purify our sensory appetite. The Lord does this because he is beginning to communicate himself to us by pure spirit.[3] Thus in sensitizing us to the more spiritual, God desensitizes us to what we need to transcend. That reversal occurs no matter how providential the creature has been in our life.

Therefore, God communicating himself to us purifies us. That communication is purgative contemplation. "Contemplation" in this context refers to the direct and immediate transforming presence of God within us purging us. By "immediate," we understand "not through any created medium." Throughout life, the Lord communes with us both directly/immediately (i.e., God-soul) and indirectly/mediately (i.e., God-creature-soul).

John sheds light on this mystery by comparing it to the consuming action of fire:

> God accomplishes the purgation of the soul by means of this dark contemplation. In it we suffer not only from emptiness and suspension of natural supports . . . but also this dark contemplation purifies us, annihilating and emptying, or consuming as does fire . . . all the affections and attachments which we have built up over an entire lifetime.[4]

In the above text, John of the Cross chooses three terms to

---

3. *Night*, I, 9, 8. See *Contemplation*, pp. 60-71; *Spiritual Journey*, pp. 104-108.
4. *Night*, II, 6, 5.

describe the purifying activity of contemplation: to annihilate
and empty, *or* — better — to consume by flame. His arrange-
ment of the contrasting conjunctions "and . . . or" implies
recognition that to annihilate can mean to destroy completely
and that to empty may be taken in an entirely negative sense.
So, lest he be misunderstood, John gives a positive interpretation to his thought by introducing the analogy of fire. That
analogy evokes the suffering which arises out of the transformative process. For in every radical change, something is
necessarily burned up.

Among the three images used, John thus indicates a
preference for the verb "to consume" precisely because of its
positive connotation:

> This purifying and loving divine light operates within us
> as does fire upon wood which transforms the wood into
> itself.[5]

B. *Interdependence of Contemplation and Purification*

A question must be posed regarding the relationship
between contemplation and purification. Is it more correct to
say that contemplation itself purifies, or to say that purification
gives way in the end to contemplation? In other words, do we
have to be purified first so that God can afterwards communicate himself directly and immediately to us, or is it the communication of God to us which effects the purgation?

In the physical order, if we have a glass full of water and
want to fill it with wine, we must empty out the water before
pouring in the wine. Do those laws apply in the spiritual realm?
Which precedes the other: contemplation or purification?

Obviously, there is reciprocal influence. Yet the positive
element clearly dominates the negative aspect, for it is contemplation which causes the purgation. The fire of divine love
burns away every attachment. God's transforming activity con-

5. *Night* II, 10, 1. In the theology of John, fire is a symbol for the Holy Spirit.

sumes whatever is un-Godlike. John explains himself this way:

> The purer and simpler divine light is in itself,the more it
> darkens and empties the soul with respect to everything
> . . . To say that seems incredible . . . Yet we grasp
> something of what it means when we realize that the
> clearer and more manifest supernatural things are in
> themselves, the more obscure they appear to our under-
> standing.[6]

Nevertheless, that explanation still does not reveal how
contemplation, or the direct and immediate activity of God
within us, purifies. John continues:

> This divine ray of contemplation, assailing the soul with
> its light, surpasses our natural light. It darkens us and
> detaches us from everything . . . we had previously
> obtained by means of natural light. It leaves us not only
> dark, but also empty in our faculties and desires, both
> spiritual and natural. Leaving us thus empty and in
> darkness, this contemplation purifies and illumines us
> with divine spiritual light. All this transpires while we
> think that we have no light and believe ourselves to be in
> darkness.[7]

In that manner, God, welling up from deep within the person,
is truly the cause of the night as mystery.

C. Causes of Purgation

If night as mystery originates with God, who or what
causes the darkness (i.e., the pain dimension) of the night?
Untold suffering emanates from the purgation integral to
the direct and immediate presence of God within us. The
source of that pain is the human condition in all its wounded-

6. *Night*, II, 8, 2. See *Night*, II, 10, 1-10.
7. *Night*, II, 8, 4. See *Night*, II, 16, 10-12.

ness, weakness and sinfulness coming under the direct influence of God. Contemplation — that is, the Lord's love welling up from within us — itself purges whatever cannot be transformed.

In all transformation, both continuity and discontinuity exist. Something endures beyond, while something else is broken off and left behind. God directly effects all dimensions of this mystery: the forging ahead, the breaking loose and the letting go. Nothing befalls us — not even sin — that God does not somehow make serve our metamorphosis in love (Rm 8:28-39).

In the context of the dark night of sense, John of the Cross furnishes three impressive examples of how God draws forth good from very painful experiences. These he calls the trials and storms of sense. They are (1) "the spirit of fornication" which assails us with an onslaught of concupiscible desires and fantasies; (2) the "spirit of blasphemy" which directs intense irascibility against God and loved ones; and (3) the "spirit of dizziness" which frequently manifests itself in the form of severe scruples and seemingly insoluble perplexities.[8]

John asserts that it really is "God who sends these storms and trials in this night and purification of the senses." The Lord does this "so that having been chastened and buffeted in that way, our senses and faculties may be exercised, disposed and prepared for divine union."[9]

In John's view, therefore, it is not enough to affirm that the night is an essentially positive reality. We must also recognize that the storms integral to the night play an equally constructive role in our divinization. But how can that be? How can something so actually painful and so potentially harmful also be so good?

We experience one and the same event both as a good and as a suffering. Those storms are evil inasmuch as they are

---

8. *Night*, I, 14, 1-3. See *Contemplation*, pp. 85-89; *Spiritual Journey*, pp. 108-113.
9. *Night*, I, 14, 4.

painful onslaughts of sin truly living within us (Rm 7:17). Yet they are also an incomparable good to the degree that God uses them despite their painfulness to exercise us. Thus, when bombarded by those storms we must simultaneously resist the evil and foster the good in them. This is not only not to succumb to temptation (Mt 6:13), but also to cooperate with God in love (Rm 8:28). In that manner, we encounter the Lord's transforming power through the storms and in the midst of the anxiety they cause. We accomplish this, however, only by naked abandonment to God in faith.

It is important to note that God does not tempt us in the strict sense (Jm 1:13-14). The Lord exercises us to bring out the best in us. The trials and storms of sense emanate from ourselves. They arise from our inner being inasmuch as we have come with all our poverty and sinfulness into direct contact with the divine transforming activity within us. Thus the darkness or pain element of the night does not, strictly speaking, proceed from God but from the human condition. It springs from our inability to receive the Lord as he is in himself. We remain innately powerless in the presence of the all-loving-transcendent-immanent One. We experience our basic weakness in proportion to the force of God within us. God's transforming intimacy systematically annihilates every trace of self-centeredness. It methodically breaks down our defense mechanisms, detaching us from even our most subtle attachments.

Therefore, the phrase "God sends these storms" accentuates the divine activity within us directly divinizing and perfecting human nature. That phrase, furthermore, highlights these truths: The disproportion between creature and Creator is so immense that divine light darkens the soul. The relationship of lover and Beloved is so foreign to our egocentrism that it convulses our self-centeredness. The power of the divine presence is so intense that it leaves us with the impression that God is absent.

How do those general principles affect individual persons in their life situations? The compassionate love of the Father sees to all the particulars of each human journey in a way best suited to the transformation of each person. Divine wisdom works out with each one the duration, the intensity and the form of purgation. The darkness of the night is "in accord with the degree of union of love to which God intends to raise the soul," and in accordance with the greater or lesser amount of selfishness to be eradicated. [10]

D. *The Purpose of Detachment*

What then is the raison d'être of purification according to St. John of the Cross? Is it primarily expiation, punishment, chastisement? Or, is it rather the exigencies of transforming love? John responds this way:

> Even though this *blessed night* darkens the spirit,
>   it does so only to impart light in all things.
> And even though it humbles us and reveals our miseries,
>   it does so only to exalt us.
> And even though it empties us of everything . . .
>   it does so only that we may reach forward divinely
>   to enjoy and to taste everything in heaven and on earth,
>   while preserving a general freedom of spirit in all. [11]

The person whom God is calling to himself is a sinner. Sin and its consequences enter deeply into the mystery of our need for purification. Nonetheless, the basic purpose of the night goes much deeper than expiation. Even though other reasons may also be ascribed, [12] the raison d'être of our purification is our existential situation vis-à-vis the uncompromising demands of our passage of transforming union.

---

10. *Night*, I, 14, 5.
11. *Night*, II, 9, 1. See *Night*, II, 16,7.
12. E.g., so that the appetites themselves may attain their proper perfection and accomplishment (*Ascent*, I, 4-10); "according to the degree of union in love willed by God's mercy" (*Night*, II, 7, 3; see *Night*, I, 14, 5).

In other words, God's loving design for us is the primary source of our purgation as well as of the intensity of our night. If God had not called us to such an incomparable destiny — to be transformed in himself, to enjoy supreme happiness and freedom in him — there would be no need for such purification.

Transformation always means dying at least partially to what one loves. This dying to self must be all the more complete when we give ourselves to a One-greater-than-ourselves. Therefore, there can be no limits to the uprooting required on our journey in God. We do not just pass from one phase of development to another, as from adolescence to adulthood. Rather, we are completely and radically transformed not only to a new life, but to God's very own life and love.

That teaching appears even when John accentuates the specifically expiatory aspect of purgation. For instance, after citing Job 19:21: "Have pity on me . . . because the hand of the Lord has touched me," John comments:

> How amazing and how pitiful it is that the weakness and woundedness of the soul are such that it experiences the gentle and light hand of God so heavy and contrary to it. The Lord only touches it, and does so mercifully without pressing it down or weighing upon it. God does this in order to pour out his graces upon the soul, not to punish it. [13]

CHAPTER 10

FAITH AND RECEPTIVITY
IN RELATION TO THE NIGHT

To enter a recovery process and to persevere in it requires an ever intensifying act of faith. The addicted, codependent or attached person lets go control of others and self as well as gives up the avoidance of pain at any cost. S/he surrenders to God, hopeful that the Lord's loving care will provide the courage to continue forward. That movement is a quantum leap into the unknown. The recovering person voluntarily relinquishes what appears sure, gratifying and safe for darkness, aridity and mystery.

The role of faith in the process of transformation remains without doubt one of St. John of the Cross's greatest contributions to spiritual theology. With regard to this vast and complex subject, we limit our observations to only one aspect — faith in relation to purgation.

A. *Faith and the Dark Night*

At the beginning of *The Ascent of Mount Carmel* (I, 2, 1), the Mystical Doctor presents an overview of the process of spiritualization which he compares to a night journey:

> The passage of the soul to divine union is called night for
> three reasons. First, because of its point of departure
> [which is the innate poverty of the soul]. Second, because
> of faith which is the means or road which we must travel to
> reach union. Third, because of the Goal of the journey —
> God.

Faith links the various phases of the journey. Faith is the
thread which weaves together the diverse elements of the
night. Faith is that by which, in which and through which the
pilgrim advances, reaches consummate union and is
transformed.

In a text from *The Dark Night of the Soul* (I, 11, 4), John of
the Cross explicates the role of faith in purgation, while allud-
ing to imagery from the Sermon on the Mount (Mt 7:14):

> The "narrow gate" is the night of sense wherein the soul is
> stripped so that, grounded in faith, it can continue on
> through the night. That faith, however, is foreign to
> everything sensory. Then, having passed through the
> gate, the soul proceeds along the "straight road" which is
> the night of spirit. The soul enters this second night in
> order to journey to God in pure faith which is the means
> whereby it is divinized.

Faith and love unite us with God. Nonetheless, faith in
the Sanjuanist perspective is dark and purifying even as it
transforms. Moreover, the darker it is, the more completely it
unifies. We shall never understand the inner dynamics of the
night until we grasp something of the purifying role of faith in
the process.

Faith as a unifying and purging principle is a myriad of
paradoxes.

(1) *The Dialectic of Faith*

Faith is the fundamental cause of the night, while remaining our only effective guide through it. Stanzas 3, 4 and 5 of the

poem *In a Dark Night* illustrate especially well that mystery:

> In this *blessed night,*
> In secret, when no one saw me
> And I could see nothing
> Without light or guide
> Save that which burned in my heart (Stanza 3).

There comes a point in the night when literally everything goes dark. Reason, common sense and intuition no longer serve as effective guides. Not even spiritual direction is satisfying. All that remains at this time is the flame of faith, hope and love which burn unremittingly in the innermost recesses of our being. They are "like a fire burning in my heart, imprisoned in my bones" (Jr 20:9).

> This guided me
> More surely than the light of noonday
> To a place where he awaited me
> — Him whom I knew so well —
> A place where no one appeared (Stanza 4).

This intensely obscure faith guides us through the perplexities of the night with a peace deeper than anything the certitudes of conventional wisdom could ever furnish. There was a time when we thought we knew our Beloved very well. We were sure of ourselves and sure of God. We assumed that the Lord was just around the next corner. Arriving there, however, we discover that he is still further up ahead. Moreover, we become less and less certain about anyone or anything. Each experience of being drawn closer to Christ is different from the previous one. Each encounter is more mysterious, more faith-laden, more obscure to our mental powers and senses. He whom we thought we knew so well is simply no longer there. The true God is infinitely beyond . . .

O night that guides me!
O night more lovely than the dawn!
O night that united
Beloved with lover,
Lover transformed in Beloved! (Stanza 5)

The overpowering darkness of faith becomes itself the source of incomparable peace and strength. Faith is both the guide to and the agent of transforming union.

Faith is both light and night. It darkens by virtue of its overwhelming brilliance — like being blinded by looking directly at the sun.[1]

As divine light, faith simultaneously illumines and purifies. In fact, it purifies by illuminating, since it illumines by way of kenosis (Ph 2:7). That is, it reveals who God is not, and it enlightens us regarding our own inner poverty together with the innate limitation of every created being.

Faith as divine light is not of itself obscure, even though its overwhelming force produces an obscuring effect within us. Thus, nothing created can adequately convey it: The eye has not seen, the ear has not heard — it has not so much as entered our imagination who God is in himself (1 Cor 2:9).

(2) *The Constructive Darkness of Faith*

As faith and the night intensify, they progressively eradicate in us all attachments. Through a process of elimination, the true God is revealed. For by letting go all that the Lord is not, we come to experience him more mysteriously "face to face" and thereby live more fully (Gn 32:31). Nevertheless, this mystical communion between God and the soul in faith causes an even more poignant darkness. The Lord is unmistakably experienced as nothing — *nada* — that can be grasped, held on to, comprehended in any human fashion. God is truly the Ineffable, the Inexpressible, the "I-don't-know-what" of *The Spiritual Canticle* (Stanza 7).

1. See *Ascent*, II, 3, 1-6.

The darkness of faith is a necessary and providential condition for total abandonment to God. Ultimately, that condition wrenches every trace of egocentrism from us. Obviously, darkness as such does not cause abandonment in faith. God alone is the cause of faith and of its intensification. Yet the obscurity resulting from the encounter of our inner poverty with divine light is the condition *sine qua non* for true surrender.

In other words, to the degree that a given creature is not affected by the obscurity of faith, we tend instinctively to cling to him, her or it. It is as if that creature were a ray of sensory light in an otherwise dark and mysterious tunnel. This happens for reasons profoundly entrenched within the human psyche. We spontaneously resist obscurity and seek what we consider certain, clear and comfortable. Darkness, however, elicits a positive response from us. For the less we can see, grasp, attach ourselves to, the more we necessarily plunge into the mystery of the divine Person up ahead. To cling is to reach behind, to hold on to something or someone. Faith is sheer leap forward; pure risk in God. Thus, faith increases in proportion to the intensity of the darkness of the night, up to and including death itself. Death is our final leap into total darkness. And yet, in death we end up in total Light.

In that manner, faith conceals God, while uniting us to him.[2] Faith is the lifeblood of purgative transformation and contemplation.[3]

Faith is God's gift. It is that which the Lord bestows on us, enabling us to respond to his initiative. The most salvific response that we can offer is commitment — the return gift of ourselves to God.

The sayings of Jesus and the writings of St. Paul are replete with declarations to this effect:

Faith is the commitment
  of that which is deepest and most ineffable in our personhood

2. See *Ascent*, II, 4, 1-8; *Night*, I, 11, 4.
3. See *Ascent*, II, 10, 4.

to that which is deepest and most mysterious in the personhood of
God — Father, Son and Spirit.

The Gospel consistently requires that the authentic disciple
not only believe *what* Jesus proclaims, but especially that s/he
believe *in* Christ himself: "Do you believe in the Son of Man?"
(Jn 9:35). The difference is that of believing some-thing and of
believing *in* some-one. It is the difference between merely
accepting the veracity of another and fully committing oneself
to the other.

Therefore, as belief in another, faith (together with love)
constitutes the basis of all interpersonal relationships, transformation and union. In that sense, faith is necessarily obscure
since it is commitment to that which is truly most *mysterious* in
the Other. In that sense, also, faith is loving response more
than intellectual assent.

> Faith is gift as well as commitment.
> Faith is both light and night.
> Faith guides and conceals, illumines and darkens.
> Faith strips us of everything, while uniting us with God.

The Lord wells up from within us gently, drawing us
forward. God gives himself, communicating himself without
ever being exhausted. Faith thus empties us in such a way that
nothing precise or specific remains to which we can cling.
What is left is All, who completely possesses us without ever
being totally possessed. God does not come to fill a void. He
was always there. Everything that is not God has become in/by
faith *nada*.

B. Receptivity: Embracing the Night

As we shall see in the next section, Pierre Teilhard de
Chardin consistently uses the noun *passivité(s)* to denote our
attitude of receptivity toward God's transforming and purifying

activity within us. Although the corresponding noun *pasividad* exists in Spanish, John of the Cross rarely uses it. He does, however, employ often the adjective *pasivo(a)* and the adverb *pasivamente* in the traditional mystical sense of loving receptivity to God.

In English, the noun "passivity" conjures up in the minds of many people laziness, inertness, unresponsiveness, indifference, apathy — all of which are diametrically opposed to the dynamic acquiescence of the soul to the divine presence within it. For that reason, we prefer the term "receptivity" in this context.

Whatever the expression, the leitmotiv of all John's teaching remains this: Everything that is done in us to divinize us is done by God. The most effective way we cooperate with God in that process is by receiving the Lord's transforming and purifying activity with faith, in hope and love. We let it be done. We also contribute actively to the process by doing what we believe God may be indicating.

To illustrate some of the many faces of receptivity, we highlight two passages from the Mystical Doctor.

(1) Padecer: *To Undergo*

The verb *padecer* (also used as a noun) means to suffer, to endure, to undergo. John of the Cross frequently uses the word to stress the excellence of loving receptivity:

> Another reason we pass securely through the night is because we advance *padeciendo*. The way of *padecer* is safer and more beneficial than experiencing God or the things of God through enjoyment or activity. This is so because, first, in *el padecer* the Lord supplies the ability, whereas in enjoyment and activity we exercise our weaknesses and imperfections. Second, in *el padecer* we are exercised and . . . purified, made wiser and more prudent.[4]

4. *Night*, II, 16, 9. See *Contemplation*, p. 113.

Undergoing pain and tribulation with a faith-imbued attitude does, therefore, contribute positively to our pursuit of a qualitative life. The Prayer of Serenity, so integral to the Twelve-Step Program of recovery from addiction and codependency beautifully captures the dynamics of *padecer*:

> God grant me
>> the serenity to accept the things I cannot change,
>> the courage to change the things I can,
>> and the wisdom to know the difference.

(2) *Passionate Love and Receptivity*

Loving both the Lord and those dear to us is integral to the process of remaining receptive to God's purgative activity:

> [During the night] the human spirit experiences itself intensely and passionately in love . . . Moreover, since this love is from God, it is more passive than active, generating in us passionate affection. Because it already possesses certain fruits of union with God, that love participates to some extent in those properties which make it more the actions of God than of us. Those properties are received in us passively. What we do is consent to them.[5]

For St. John of the Cross, "passivity" is used in contradistinction to "activity." This is especially the case when remaining expectantly receptive to God's transforming and purifying activity within us. We cooperate optimally with the Lord by consciously and lovingly — hence, voluntarily — letting God do in us and with us whatever he wills. In that surrender, the Lord increases our capacity to love him, ourselves, others and all creation.

In the context of loving receptivity, therefore, passivity derives its ultimate meaning from passion/passionate. Thus,

---

5. *Night*, II, 11, 2. See *Night* I, 10, 6.

"passive" signifies being enflamed with love, becoming fully alive in Christ:

> I live now, no longer I,
> but Christ lives in me (Gal 2:20).

Recovery from addiction, codependency and attachments ultimately includes letting the passion of God's love heal the last vestiges of the woundedness which gave rise to those abuses in the first place. Thus, we in turn can love with consummate freedom. In the final analysis, passionate love for God, self, others and creation is the crux of recovery.

SOLITUDE
IN RELATION TO THE DARK NIGHT

According to St. John of the Cross, both involvement with creation and passage in faith through the night are essential to recovering and to continuing to discover our true self in Christ. In that way, detachment and purgation are necessary conditions for learning to maturely love ourselves, others, creation and God. Those aspects of recovery, however, need to be examined also in relation to solitude.

We use the word "solitude" in a very specific sense.

First, we distinguish *solitude* from *isolation*. The two are as different as light from darkness.

Isolation is the aloneness which results from being enmeshed in self-centeredness. It is a characteristic of addiction, codependency and attachment which tends to drive people out of their mind. Isolation connotes regression and closing in upon self, hence: selfishness, self-pity and self-complacency. Isolation causes one to shun involvements and activities with others in order to block out the light. Frequently accompanying isolation are loneliness, or the feeling of being cut off, and boredom, which arises from overindulgence in creatures. Isolated persons are disgruntled, despondent, dissatisfied loners.

Solitude, on the other hand, is the aloneness experienced in encountering one's true self. It is a characteristic of detachment and maturity which drives people into becoming fully who they are destined to be. It connotes being drawn into self by God in order to empty self of selfishness. Solitude is the basis of personalism and altruism. It is invigorating risk and forward leap. It is being alone in order to let light break forth from within. Usually associated with solitude are the aloneness and the aridity which we undergo as our created finite heart is being opened to uncreated infinite Love. Persons at home in solitude are self-assured, self-reliant, self-giving individuals.

Second, solitude is both a *psychological* and a *theological* reality. In the psychological sphere, the accent falls on being alone with ourselves holistically, facing all observable aspects of our concrete life situation. That experience opens out to the theological realm. There, we allow solitude to draw us to its deepest and most intensely holistic dimension — loving communion with God dwelling within us. The psychological and the theological dimensions of solitude blend and interact so that one cannot exist beyond an elementary degree without the other. Ultimately, therefore, solitude designates our ability to stand alone before God. We are so at home with ourselves that we yearn to remain face-to-face with our Lord, Redeemer and Beloved.

Continuing recovery needs support systems. Yet, in order to advance beyond a certain point of maturity, recovery requires also a capacity to be peacefully and holistically alone with ourselves and with God in us. The detachment and the purgation integral to recovery unfold in solitude, and they open us to increasing solitude. The solitary dimension of recovery comprises three interrelating and interacting factors: physical aloneness, interior aloneness and the aloneness of being a unique person.

A. *Physical Solitude*

By physical solitude we understand being alone with God, without the mediation or presence of any other person.

The Mystical Doctor perceives the value of physical aloneness in its ability to free us to be more attentive both to our authentic selves and to God within us.[1] Lovers need to be alone with each other in order to commune together more intimately.

The integration of exterior solitude with the other aspects of our life follows the example of Jesus:

> Who habitually sought out deserted places
> in order to be alone and pray (Lk 5:16);
> Who, before choosing the Apostles,
> spent the whole night in solitary prayer to God (Lk 6:12);
> Who, after dismissing the crowds,
> went up into the hills by himself to pray,
> so that, when evening came,
> he was still there alone (Mt 14:23).

In physical solitude, we give ourselves the space and the time to tap the richness of our deepest selves. We put aside for a while our usual activities, interactions and involvements to listen to our inner being. In that stance, we sense our physical, spiritual, mental and emotional boundaries in distinction to those of other people.

Until we can stand being with ourselves, we cannot qualitatively be with God, other persons or creation. Moreover, some external aloneness is necessary to perform tasks which facilitate recovery: reflection, study, prayer, creative leisure, journaling, rest, etc.

B. *Interior Solitude*

Interior solitude embraces our inner world of experience. It denotes being attentive to our thoughts, feelings, perceptions and imaginations. It invites us to identify and to own our hopes and fears, our giftedness and poverty, our wholeness and woundedness.

---

1. See *Contemplation*, pp. 59, 68, 97-99, 126-131.

Awareness of that solitude opens us to the mysterious depths of our personhood. It thrusts us on a pilgrimage toward our inmost being — a journey through valleys and mountains, darkness and light, turmoil and peace. Interior solitude, although luring us along a winding path, ultimately brings us to the reality of our true self where:

> I live now, no longer I,
>   but Christ lives in me (Gal 2:20).

Thus, interior solitude designates abiding communion with the Beloved in our inmost depths, no matter where we are or what we are doing. That intimacy is possible because of the indwelling Trinity — the mystery of the inner life and relatedness of Father, Son and Spirit truly existing within and animating each of us.

Ordinarily, it takes some time before we experience solitude in such a positive vein. Generally, we fear what we know exists within us: hurt, pain, shame, etc. and we fear even more what still remains to be revealed. We cringe at not only discovering more woundedness, but also uncovering more giftedness and the immense responsibilities that may entail. Therefore, out of dread, we resist our interior solitude or flee it altogether through a myriad of diversions, including addictions, codependency and attachments.

(1) *Interior Solitude and Involvement with Creation*

Interior solitude is a matter of the heart. It persists within us not only when we are physically alone, but also while we are actively engaged with other persons.

What John of the Cross describes as the wound of love is but a concentration of interior solitude. The experience of our inability to be completely satisfied by anyone or anything except God alone thrusts us into this inner desert. Our encounter with God within personal and nonpersonal creation, as well as directly within us, leaves us yearning to experience his unabated fullness.

Thus inner solitude often feels like emptiness, aridity, absence. It manifests itself as hungering, thirsting, pining for a Power-greater-than-oneself. Whatever the symbol, solitude of heart is the abode of deepening intimacy with Father, Son and Spirit.

Interior solitude is a prime consequence of detachment. It is the condition in which we find ourselves as we loosen our tenacious grip on the creatures in our life. It denotes the inner freedom which enables us to maturely love God, ourselves and creation. It is the gift which gradually flowers as we let go all for the sake of Jesus and the gospel (Mk 10:29).

By relinquishing our disordered desires and surrendering our fixations, we carve out an empty space in ourselves. That void is not, however, negative emptiness. It is rather like a delicate fragrance whose subtle presence permeates the atmosphere.

(2) *Intensification of Interior Solitude During the Dark Night*

The dark night of the soul is a process characterized by more radical detachment, coupled with more accentuated aloneness in God.

In the night of sense, our assertive and pleasure-seeking appetites are progressively purged of their immaturities. Aggressivity becomes tempered. We act and respond more out of conviction and a sense of mission than out of rage or fear. We deal constructively with our frustrations without needing to repress them. We delight in pleasures without having to suffocate them. We enjoy what we like without being driven to drain it of life. We experience people and nature as from God and to him without turning them into objects of self-centered gratification. That maturation is accompanied by "an inclination to remain alone and in quiet" contemplation of God. [2]

2. *Night*, I, 9, 6. See *Spiritual Journey*, pp. 41, 50-52, 99-124.

In the night of spirit, the Lord's activity is directed toward the transformation and purgation of faith, hope and love. We find no support or guide except in those virtues, but purified in ways we never imagined.[3] For example: As we are drawn into intensifying faith in the person of Jesus, we discover diminishing reassurance from the myriad of beliefs which characterized our earlier religiosity. The relatively serene hope in God of previous years is giving way to an extremely restless goading toward the ineffable One-Thing-Necessary (Lk 10:41). The former quasi-romantic affection for God in which we had so delighted is gradually changing into a love for Father, Son and Spirit which is so unemotional that we wonder agonizingly whether it exists at all. Solitude during the night of spirit consists primarily of abiding in the darkness and emptiness caused by increasing faith, hope and love.

In the tranquil night of spiritual espousal, the stripping and the solitude are such that the person can almost taste God becoming all in all. Thus there emerges a radically transformed way of relating to oneself and to creatures. John of the Cross writes of a "sounding solitude" to describe the vibrant cosmic dimension of this communion with all creation in the Beloved.[4]

In the serene night of spiritual marriage, the detachment and the solitude of soul reach their peak this side of personal death/resurrection. At this culminating and consummating point in the spiritual journey:

> The soul lives in solitude
> And in solitude has forevermore built her nest.
> In solitude her Beloved alone guides her,
> He who also bears
> In solitude the wound of Love.[5]

Throughout our earthly sojourn, intensifying detachment and increasing aloneness with God characterize authentic

3. See *Spiritual Journey*, pp. 163-168.
4. See *Canticle*, Stanza 15; *Spiritual Journey*, pp. 201-211.
5. *Canticle*, Stanza 35. See *Spiritual Journey*, 212-226.

intimacy with ourselves and with significant people. Detachment and solitude form more and more the crux of every
in-depth relationship and each meaningful interaction. Detachment and solitude are, therefore, at opposite poles from
withdrawal, isolation or rugged individualism. As manifestations of the presence within us of a Power-greater-than-
ourselves, they guide us beyond selfishness and woundedness
to communion with God and with creation in God.

We need to accept deepening aloneness in order to
establish personal boundaries and to respect those of other
people. Befriending our inner solitude enables us to be
ourselves, while truly giving ourselves in loving service to God
and others.

(3) *Interior Solitude in Relation to Twelve-step Recovery Programs*

Following a twelve-step program of recovery thrusts the
person in the direction of intensifying detachment and increasing solitude of heart.

The very first step of that program consists in a solitary
soul-wrenching experience. As addicted or codependent
persons, we realize that our life has become unmanageable and
that we are unable to change the situation by willpower alone.
In taking that step, we embark on an inner journey. We begin
to experience feelings which we had denied or repressed. We
start identifying personal values and convictions. We initiate
getting in touch with our deepest aspirations. We see how we
sabotage our efforts to find happiness and wholeness.

Undertaking a fearless moral inventory and continuing to
be dauntlessly honest with ourselves (steps 4 and 10) also
require solitude of heart. Facing our inner aloneness opens to us
the truth of ourselves and of our behavior. It dispels illusions
and disarms defenses. It enables us to stand peacefully in
God's light. It calls us to personal responsibility and accounta-
bility. It reveals to us the inner pain which can be destructive
or transformative, depending on how we deal with it.

Interior solitude opens us to an ever deepening experience of a Power-greater-than-ourselves (step 2). Hopeful acknowledgment of powerlessness and unmanageability forces us to trust in Someone. It makes us surrender our woundedness to Another's care. That letting go becomes actualized in readiness to let God remove character defects (steps 6 and 7). Recovery commits us also to consistent prayer and meditation (step 11). As we enter into a deepening relationship with ourselves and God, we also learn to relate more lovingly to the significant persons in our lives (steps 4, 5, 8, 9, 10 and 12).

C. The Solitude of Being a Unique Person

Recovery according to twelve-step programs is based on and geared toward a "spiritual awakening" (step 12). That awakening means reclaiming and developing our true self, our unique identity.

For most people, that consciousness begins to dawn as a result of involvements, interactions and interpersonal relationships. After it has matured, however, awareness of ourselves as singular persons is authenticated and intensified in solitude. The yearning for more physical aloneness and increased interior solitude both flows from and redounds to the experience of our unique personhood come face-to-face with God. In that stance, we pray with the psalmist and with Mary:

You created my inmost self, O Lord;
   you knit me together in my mother's womb.
I praise you because
   I am so awesomely and wonderfully made (Ps 139:13-14).
My innermost being rejoices in God . . .
   for the Lord has done great things in me (Lk 1:47-49).

The mystery of each person is God's handiwork. The Lord not only gifts us with ourselves, but also from our inception begins in us a process of forming and recreating us in the image of the Trinity (Gn 1:27; Col 3:10). The gift of self is that of a unique individual becoming transformed in God. John of the Cross describes the final stages of that metamorphosis in these terms:

> So complete a union exists that the qualities of God and those of the soul become one in participant transformation. The soul appears to be more God than soul. Indeed, it is God by participation. Yet, its being remains distinct from God.[6]

The dark night of the soul is the flip-side of transforming union. Throughout the night, the Lord continues his work of creating us and of revealing to us who we are. In that manner, the Father bestows on us our full identity in his Son through the Spirit.

The dark night then is a symbol for undergoing whatever is necessary in order to become fully who God calls me to be. To pass through the night causes me to enter more deeply the solitude of who I am in God. It requires assuming responsibility for the singular destiny that is mine. Journey through the night presupposes owning the ever increasing solitariness of my individual self, of my life and of my death.

Experiencing the solitude of my unique personhood, therefore, means accepting, rejoicing in and fostering my singular individuality in such a way that it leads to the consciousness that only in God do I "live and move and have my being" (Ac 17:28). That very solitariness then becomes the catalyst for deepening communion with all creation in God.

D. Summary

Throughout this section we have examined two interconnected aspects of the mystical theology of St. John of the Cross: the positive role of creatures in the process of sanctification,

6. *Ascent*, II, 5, 7. See *Contemplation*, pp. 13-20.

and the positive thrust of the night. Both aspects highlight the
vital link between detachment and the process of transforming
love. Several conclusions flow from those considerations:

(1) God is revealed and communicated to us most deeply
in the kenosis (Ph 2:7) of ourselves and of everything created.
That truth becomes actualized for us through our personal
incorporation into the mystery of Christ's incarnation, death
and resurrection. In light of that mystery:

> The positive role of creation is
>   to open our hearts to the Uncreated.
> The positive role of the finite is
>   to point us beyond itself to the Infinite.

That opening to and pointing beyond are effected by way
of *nada*, for God is "no-thing." The Lord is nothing created.

(2) Kenosis is truly a process, a development. We do not,
strictly speaking, enter into it. Rather, we are permeated and
swept along by it. The most efficacious way to cooperate with
the movement is to let go in order to let God unite us with him.

(3) One of the great paradoxes related to addictions,
codependencies and attachments is the illusion of control.
Addicts think that by means of their addiction they have
mastery over the pain they so desperately try to avoid. In
reality, however, they are utterly out of control. Their addiction enslaves them. For that reason, the process of recovery
requires three breakthroughs:

(a) breaking the tyranny of the addiction by gaining
    self-control;
(b) letting go control of one's destiny in view of loving
    receptivity to God;
(c) letting God take total control of ourselves and of our
    lives.

We cannot let go some attachments and defense mechanisms
until the Lord breaks our grip on them. Willpower alone — no

matter how well-developed — does not always suffice. Some attachments, moreover, are not effectively broken except in death.

(4) Once a person has broken with chemical dependencies, s/he has to deal with a host of emotional and mental subjugations. When they are addressed, the individual must still reckon with a myriad of attachments to persons, situations and things. The task is so mind-boggling that the weary pilgrim cries out with St. Paul:

What a wretch I am!
Who will rescue me from this endless quagmire? (Rm 7:24).

Yet, also with St. Paul, we abandon ourselves to divine love:

Thanks be to God!
Transformation is through Jesus Christ our Lord! (Rm 7:25).

(5) Another paradox is that addicts, codependent and attached persons pursue those courses because they are basically dissatisfied with creation. Creatures cannot fulfill all their needs, yet they continue to demand that creatures do so. *Dissatisfaction* — an inherently negative, debilitating experience — leads to addictions, codependencies and attachments. On the other hand, *the inability to be satisfied* — an innately positive, hope-engendering experience, although sometimes excruciatingly painful — leads to God in, through and beyond creatures. That is the quintessence of the wound of love.

(6) Addictions, codependency and attachments indicate fixation of the will. Persons so enslaved have become detached from their true self and from God. Recovery, therefore, leads to at-homeness with self and attachment to the Lord. It directs the person toward letting one's will become vulnerable to the divine transforming and purifying activity within it.

(7) Solitude is essential to the recovery process. We need the time, the space and the leisure to face our inner pains and

fears so as consciously to let them go — or, at least, to want to
let them go. Our resistances are formidable. Solitude forces us
to encounter our true self — not only our weaknesses and
immaturities, but also the giftedness of our unique identity in
Christ Jesus. Solitude teaches us that God loves us in our
woundedness and is working with us to restore wholeness:

> So, we rejoice in our sufferings, because we are convinced
>   that suffering produces perseverance,
>   and perseverance builds character,
>   and character leads to hope.
> Now, our hope is founded on this inscrutable mystery . . .:
> God poured out his love into our hearts . . .
> Indeed, when we were still powerless,
>   Christ died to redeem us from our ungodliness . . .
> God demonstrated unequivocally his love for us in this:
>   while we were still sinners,
>   Christ offered up his life to save us (Rm 5:3-8).

PIERRE TEILHARD DE CHARDIN
ON DETACHMENT

CHAPTER 12

PASSIVITIES OF EXISTENCE

In the first section of this book we summarized the general understanding of addiction, codependency and attachment. In the second section, we presented the theological underpinnings according to St. John of the Cross for recovery from them. In this third section, we complement that theology with the evolutionary perspective of Pierre Teilhard de Chardin, S.J. (1881-1955).

Much of what the Mystical Doctor referred to as the "dark night of the soul" Teilhard calls: "passivities of existence," "passivities of growth," "passivities of diminishment" and "receptivity of a superior order." By those expressions, he designates our receptivity toward God as we undergo his transforming and purifying activity within us and all around us. That receptive stance underlies the Twelve-Step Program for recovery from addiction and codependency. It permeates also the process of detachment.

In *The Divine Milieu* (1927, p. 75), Teilhard describes in the broadest possible terms the meaning of receptivity:

> That which is not done by us
> is by definition received in us.

Thus our passivities constitute a complex of reality within us and around us, but without us and oftentimes in spite of us.

In English, passivity is frequently associated with unresponsiveness, inactivity, indolence, apathy, unconcern, etc. Those pejorative connotations could not be further from Teilhard's mind. He rather links "passivity" with the verb "to pass into" as in: Christ's energy passing into us; and with the adverb "passionately" as in: being more intensely in love with Jesus. Thus Teilhard's theology of receptivity — as it underpins recovery from addiction, codependency and attachment — profoundly relates to his Christology, especially to the passion of Jesus:

> [For] when we suffer, two things happen:
>   (1) *Christum patimur* [we suffer/undergo Christ].
>   (2) *Christus in nobis patitur* [Christ suffers in us].
> Thus, Christ and I suffer together (*com-patimur*).[1]

Studying Teilhard chronologically — that is, beginning with his letters to his parents in 1905 (age 24) and with his first major essays in 1916 (age 35) — we see that he struggled continuously with a certain codependency and with the practical implications of detachment. Even though his parents were loving and his childhood relatively happy, in some respects Pierre grew up in a dysfunctional familial, societal and ecclesial system. That dysfunctionality centered principally around the following dichotomies:

> matter versus spirit;
> science versus religion;
> love of the world versus love of God;
> body versus soul;
> the ordinary things of life versus the sacred;
> natural versus "supernatural";
> intense involvement in creation versus detachment.

In other contexts, that dysfunctionality focused around these issues:

1. *Journal*, 28 Feb. 1919.

academic freedom versus blind obedience;
revelation of God in creation versus Church's magisterium;
inner conviction versus hierarchical imposition;
need to always search further versus conformity;
daring exploration versus tutiorism (i.e., always
    opting for what others consider the "safest" moral
    or legal way);
constantly moving forward versus maintaining the status quo;
prophetic element of the Church versus the institutional
    element.

Teilhard suffered each of those polarities as either/or situations instead of as both/and. The systems in which he was reared led him to experience them as seemingly irreconcilable opposites rather than as poles in a dialectic. He searched an entire lifetime to overcome both in theory and in practice those dysfunctionalities. Thus his theology of detachment flows not only from an evolutionary world view, but also from his personal struggle and development. Therefore, by way of example, we highlight some of those experiences in the following chapters.[2]

The term *passivité(s)* is found most frequently in Teilhard's essays and correspondence between his tour of duty during World War I (1916) and the composition of *The Divine Milieu* (1927) after being exiled to China. The word occurs principally in contexts which touch upon the mystery of interior detachment or which involve some painful incident. Often, Teilhard employs the expression *les passivités* without a qualifier. In certain contexts, however, he does specify the kind of receptivity. Our presentation is arranged according to the basic specifications which he uses:

Passivities of Existence (chapters 12 and 13);
Passivities of Growth and Diminishment (chapters 14 and 15);
Receptivity of a Superior Order (chapters 16 and 17).

2. We believe that there was some dysfunctionality in the life of St. John of the Cross, too. However, since he left us so little autobiographical testimony, we did not refer to the lived experience dimension of John's theology of detachment except for the mention of his prison ordeal in Chapter 8.

A. A Medic in Trench Warfare

Teilhard was ordained a priest in 1911. From 1912 to the onset of World War I, he pursued doctoral studies in science at the Museum of Natural History in Paris. In December 1914, Pierre was drafted into the French army as a stretcher-bearer. His infantry regiment, made up primarily of North African Zouaves, suffered severe casualties throughout the four years of the war, but especially during the battle of Verdun where they spent most of 1916 and during the counteroffensive of the Marne in 1918. Teilhard himself was not even wounded. However, two of his younger brothers as well as several close Jesuit friends were killed in the service of their country. Having led a rather sheltered life till the age of thirty-three, the war represented for Pierre a horrifying baptism by fire into the violent world of global conflict. It was for him also a time of profound spiritual awakening and extensive literary output.

Teilhard uses the expression *les passivités de l'existence* for the first time in a letter from the front to his cousin Marguerite.[3] In that letter, he discerns two essential components of our contribution to the Real: (1) that "effort without which a certain portion of being would never be actualized," and (2) those "powerful energies which force even our staunchest resistances to bend before them and acknowledge their mastery." The efficacy of those energies derives from the fact that they make us undergo "the creative and formative action of God who alone has the power to detach us from ourselves." Those passivities "establish in us something that is not from us." Teilhard epitomizes his sentiments this way:

> O, the joy of experiencing the activity of the Other within us! That is precisely what makes the passivities of existence so delicate and so worthy of adoration, since through them God asserts his primacy over us.

In other words, there are two complementary components of our contribution to reality — that is, to the actual world in

3. See *MM* (28 Dec. 1916), pp. 156-158. The same for the quotations which follow.

which we live. They are personal effort and the passivities of existence. These passivities are energies — indeed, a vast complex of influences — which overwhelm us, forcing us contrary to some of our most innate tendencies to yield to a Power-greater-than-ourselves. These passivities constitute an essential element of the creative and re-creative action of God, since they constitute the only force powerful enough to detach us from the vortex of egocentrism. They impart to us something of the Real which we could not otherwise attain.

The phrase "passivities of existence" refers to the transforming and purifying activity of God deep within the human person. That phrase accentuates the purgative aspect of the Lord's action, for in undergoing God more intensely we necessarily also suffer more acutely than ever our inner poverty. The word *passivité* denotes our fundamental disposition of receptivity and availability with respect to the divine presence within us and all around us. Because God asserts his primacy over us through these passivities, they are worthy of "adoration"; that is, of voluntary acquiescence. Furthermore, they produce profound joy even though they are accompanied by suffering proportionate to our resistance, immaturity and selfishness.

The qualifier "of existence" means "the Real" in the sense of the real world as well as the real Way, the real Truth, the real Life (Jn 14:6):

At the outset of his/her spiritual journey, the perception of God present in all things presupposed in the searcher an intense *zest* for what is *Real.*

A little later on, collaboration with God active in everything forced the pilgrim to develop as wide a *consciousness* as possible, again of the *Real.*

Now that s/he is progressing further into the immanent God, the searcher is as committed as anyone to an unremitting *fulfillment,* always of the *Real.*

That can mean only one thing: The passionate desire for union with God forces the sojourner to give created entities *their maximum degree of reality* —

> whether in his/her knowledge of and love for them, or in their proper being.
>
> Thus, out of the depths of his/her vision — which some call a dream — the interiorly maturing pilgrim is *a supreme Realist*.[4]

The determinative "of existence" indicates also that the human person exists in order to become more. In the light of Christ, that becoming is not just toward a nondescript "more." It denotes transforming union in God, by God, and thus the full undergoing of the Power-greater-than-ourselves. The very fact that we exist carries with it a destiny which completely transcends whatever we could become of ourselves. We receive not only our initial act of existence, but also the entire complexity of re-creative energies which comprise transformation.

B. *Teilhard's Interior Vision*

At the age of thirty-six, Teilhard made a concise first attempt to trace the genesis of his "interior vision" in an essay entitled *My Universe* (1918).[5] That vision comprises "the earliest and most essential characteristics of my 'view of the World' together with the successive stages of my complex inner attitude." Reflecting on that fact, he observes:

> "As far back as I can remember (even before the age of ten), I can distinguish clearly within myself the presence of a dominant passion: the passion for the Absolute . . . It expressed itself in terms of an insatiable need to rest unceasingly in Something tangible and definitive. Moreover, I sought everywhere for that blissful object. In fact, the history of my interior life can be said to revolve around the development of this search directed as it was upon realities ever more universal and perfect.

---

4. "The Mystical Milieu" (1917) in *Writings*, p. 139.
5. *HM*, pp. 196-208. The same for many of the quotations to the end of this chapter.

Then, at the age of sixty-nine, Teilhard tried again to synthesize the major components of his inner vision in *The Heart of Matter* (1950).[6] This time, he identifies the axis of continuity in his life as "the Sense of Fullness" or his intuitive movement toward the "Cosmic Christ" — a reference to John 1:16, Ephesians 1:23 and Colossians 2:9. Those phrases delineate his quest and irresistible need for "the unique all-sufficing and necessary Reality" (cf. Lk 10:42). That need was born of the conviction that Something essential exists toward which everything else converges. Thus what Teilhard calls successively "Sense of Consistency, Cosmic Sense, Human Sense, Christic Sense" is merely the account of a gradual explication of the same essential element expressed in ever richer and more refined ways.

What exactly were some of those richer and more refined ways?

They revolve around what Teilhard termed in later life "the call of Matter," or more precisely, "the call of Something burning at the heart of Matter." Reminiscing back to the age of six, he notices that he was already a searcher. Whereas most children of that age would be lost in a world of make-believe, Pierre found himself seeking out a solitary corner of the family property in mountainous central France to "contemplate the savored existence" of his "God of Iron." Curious behavior for a little boy, wouldn't you say? And why iron, of all things? Teilhard himself smiles as he recalls those events. But he was dead serious at the time. Moreover, it was not just any piece of iron. It had to be massive and heavy — like a plow or a statue — in order to attract his "adoration." Thus, in his childish way, through the symbol of iron he sought that which must be lasting and durable — in a word: immortal. Nonetheless, to the child's despair, he realized one day that iron rusts and corrodes. It was not the Power-greater-than-himself whom his heart sought with such ardor.

That setback, however, was only momentary. For it had the effect of a catalyst forcing him to search further and

6. *HM*, pp. 14-79.

elsewhere for something more consistent. This time, rocks attracted his attention. But not just any rocks. They too had to be massive and indestructible, like those in the mountains around his home. Alas, however! Even those boulders occasionally broke loose and came crashing down into the valleys below, shattering into a thousand pieces. So he had to search still further.

In that way, Teilhard was thrust in the direction of the planetary, which in turn progressively brought him "to the vision of the Universal and the discovery of Evolution." That experience finally caused his "inner awakening" to "Cosmic Life" — that is, to a divine call emanating from the Heart of Matter; to a divine Person transforming Matter from within.

Thus, from iron to rocks to the cosmic, Teilhard's quest produced in the end "the arousing and the development of a dominant and victorious Sense of All" — of *Todo*.

In the above summary of certain thresholds in the genesis of Teilhard's interior vision, several features of the passivities of existence are striking.

First, there is his irresistible and progressive probe for more and more. That need always to explore further is within him, without being of him. Yet it remains intimately bound to his voluntary cooperation with that inner Power-greater-than-himself.

Second, each threshold crossed in pursuit of "the more" is effected within a painful detachment. That detachment proceeds from two interrelated sources: (1) from the progressive intensity of the action of God within him and (2) from the purification emanating from that transforming activity. In this manner, Teilhard is placed directly on the road toward the fullness of being-becoming.

That process deserves a more detailed examination. Three examples from Teilhard's early adult life serve to illustrate how adversity brought him directly into contact with deeper values. They are: (1) the death of his older brother Alberic, (2) his cult of inert passivities, and (3) his interior crisis during May-June 1916. We address those events in the next chapter.

CHAPTER 13

EXPERIENCING THE PASSIVITIES
OF EXISTENCE

The phrase *les passivités de l'existence* was formulated by Pierre Teilhard de Chardin during his tour of duty as a stretcher-bearer on the front lines during World War I. By that expression, he understands the complex of influences within us and around us which God uses to transform and purge us. We experience most of those passivities in a very painful manner. Yet, if we face the pain and pass through it — thus allowing the suffering to produce its constructive effect for us — even the most agonizing passivities can become catalysts for unimaginable good.

In this chapter, we present three such events from the life of Teilhard: (A) the untimely death of his idealized brother Alberic (1902), (B) the experience of a hopeless dead-end during his first contact with the East (1905-1908), (C) his terrifying despair during the battle of Verdun (1916). We round off the chapter with some concluding reflections on (D) fostering the passivities of existence.

A. *The Death of Alberic*

In his two major autobiographical essays — *My Universe* (1918) and *The Heart of Matter* (1950) — Teilhard reveals a personal horror when faced with corruptibility:

> As a child, the flesh of Our Lord seemed to me something too fragile and too corruptible . . .
>
> Pathetic despairs of a child! I discovered one fine day that iron corrodes, that steel rusts . . .
>
> As a consequence of their apparent frailty, living beings greatly disquieted and disconcerted my childhood . . .
>
> The physical-chemical instability of organic substances, and more particularly of the human body, shocked my need for consistency. [1]

In the eyes of young Pierre, everything which corrupted seemed to cease existing. Corruption and mortality equaled disappearance of being. That attitude is understandable from the perspective of a youth enthralled with life and nature. However, the setbacks caused by the decomposition of his cherished matter incited Teilhard to go through and beyond the appearances. He continued to search for the Incorruptible not exactly in matter but at the *Heart* of Matter.

It is difficult to reconstruct precisely the interior upheavals of a youth, but the thread which at that time ran through all this restlessness is undoubtedly the mystery of death. Pierre must have seen death first-hand several times during his formative years, but one death in particular wrenched him to the very core — the passing of his eldest brother Alberic in September 1902.

Teilhard's reflections on this death reach us from his teaching post in Egypt (1905-1908). In a dozen or so letters to his parents, Pierre mentions his brother. There is nostalgia and much pain, but no sign of moroseness. Teilhard speaks of his passing with ardent feeling and tenderness, as if it had a lasting effect on his life. Instead of diminishing with time, his memories seem only to increase in fondness and depth during his years of theology in England (1908-1912).

Who was Alberic for Pierre?

Alberic embodied for him the ideal big brother: hand-

1. *HM*, pp. 17-44, 197.

some, intelligent, courageous, the type of man that the younger Pierre yearned to imitate. He was a unique and living model of that consistency which Teilhard so craved. But alas! At the very apex of his manhood, Alberic was struck by a slow and pitiful emaciation that ended in death.

Such a soul-wrenching experience in Pierre's impressionable youth must have shattered a host of idols. At the age of twenty-one, he was forced to face with particular acuity these critical questions of life: What is death? Does it have a positive meaning? Does incorruptibility exist beyond what we perceive as most corruptible?

Reflection on Alberic's death in its relation to Teilhard's interior development helps us to appreciate more the following sentiments addressed from the trenches near Verdun to his childhood companion and cousin Marguerite:

> I remain faithful to my cult of the other component of the Real: That is, to the powerful energies which force our most tenacious resistances to bend before them and to acknowledge their mastery. I relished . . . the words on suffering which you sent me. Through every phrase shone the creative, formative action of God whose influence alone has the power to detach us from ourselves . . . That is precisely what makes the passivities of existence seem so delicate and worthy of adoration: Through them God asserts his primacy over us . . . The more I think of it, the more I find that death . . . is a liberation and a solace, in spite of the fact that it is so painful. [2]

B. A Dead-End: The Cult of Inert Passivities

In the above letter to Marguerite, Teilhard introduced his remarks concerning the passivities of existence by referring to his "cult" of them. By cult in this context he means "adoration"; that is, an attitude of loving submission to a Power-

---

2. *MM* (28 Dec. 1916), p. 158.

greater-than-ourselves operative within and beyond those passivities. This receptivity he distinguishes from the "cult of
passivity" which he perceives in certain Oriental movements.
The cult of passivity consists in succumbing to the "temptation
of matter," thus giving in to the inclination toward the least
effort. The latter is a false cult wrongly pursued by certain
putative mystics, especially those favoring a pantheism of
fusion and dissolution.

Teilhard knows by personal experience whereof he
speaks, for he found himself locked into a dead-end situation
in this regard. It came about this way: Pierre had grown up in a
familial and religious milieu which was staunchly dualistic
and thoroughly imbued with Jansenism — hence, dysfunctional. There was his Christian self and his "pagan" self; his
love of God and his love of the World. He wanted desperately
to serve both the Church and science. The same passion was
catapulting him simultaneously in two apparently incompatible directions. Teilhard firmly believed that they could —
indeed, must — be reconcilable. Yet, he was powerless to do
so himself. Nor could he find much help in spiritual guidance
other than the sound advice that somehow he had to continue
pursuing both as far as they might take him.

In his late twenties, Teilhard became inconsolably frustrated with the inability of the asceticism in which he had been
reared to bring about a peaceful resolution of this seemingly
interminable conflict. So, without adverting to what was happening during his three-year teaching sabbatical in Egypt
(1905-1908), he began to slip into the cult of inert passivity.
That cult consisted in sliding back and downward into dissipa-
tion, laziness and a certain self-indulgence rather than struggling forward and upward toward union in love:

> In order to be All, I must be fused with all . . . Such was
> the mystical movement to which, following so many
> Hindu poets and mystics, I was logically being driven by
> an innate, ungovernable need to attain self-fulfillment
> . . . by becoming one with the Other . . . [Indeed, I might

> have succumbed to that temptation] had not — just in the
> nick of time — the idea of Evolution sprouted up like a
> seed from within me. Whence it came, I cannot say.[3]

Thus it was the notion of Evolution — ultimately that of
Christogenesis — which freed Teilhard from his interior dilemma. Like a presence welling up within him, it dawned on
him that the detachment inherent in the process of transforming union is not a question of Matter *versus* Spirit (i.e., as if one
must cancel out the other), or even of Matter *and* Spirit (i.e., as
in parallel lines), but rather of Matter *becoming* Spirit (i.e.,
like a caterpillar being transformed into a butterfly). Spirit is
that which creation is becoming in Christ (Ep 1:10; Col 1:15-
20) its Alpha and Omega (Rv 22:13).

In this way, spiritualization is not accomplished by dematerializing oneself, but by letting Christ christify that self,
by letting his Spirit spiritualize one's Matter (Rm 7-8; 1 Cor
15). That truth underlies the passivities of existence. That is
also what makes them so worthy of adoration.

In order to escape the pain of frustration and hopeless-
ness in his life at that time, Teilhard did not turn to cocaine or
alcohol but to a cult — the cult of false passivity. Unwittingly,
he was heading toward addiction. Pierre was saved, however,
by an authentic "passivity" — that of allowing a Force, an
Energy, a new Light, to spring up from within him permeating
his soul like a Presence. That influence manifested itself in
proportion to his effort to remain receptive to it and to cooperate actively with it. Thus, he allowed his inner self to be
reshaped by the creative and formative action of a Power-
greater-than-himself.

God used that potentially disastrous situation in
Teilhard's life to teach him an invaluable lesson: namely, the
One who seeks him and for whom he yearns can never be found
in the direction of matter, but only in the direction of Spirit.
Thus:

---

3. "The Heart of Matter" (1950), in *HM*, pp. 24-29, 45-49. See *Receptivity*, pp. 71-75.

The sense of Plenitude was turned upside down in me
[during those years]. Moreover, I have followed this new
direction ever since, without ever looking back . . . It
literally spun me around in my fundamental quest for
Consistency.[4]

The death of Alberic and the ordeal of the cult of inert
passivity constituted dreadfully painful but salutary experiences which Teilhard underwent in faith. They were moments
of veritable conversion. Through them, God asserted his primacy over Pierre and intensified his search for the Power-
greater-than-himself. However, the passivity of existence
which was perhaps the most detaching (at least up to the age of
thirty-six) occurred during his terrifying involvement in the
battle of Verdun.

C. Teilhard's Interior Crisis of May-June 1916

At this period of his life, Teilhard was corresponding with
his cousin Marguerite two or three times a week. Moreover, he
was writing in his *Journal* almost daily. Then, all of a sudden,
we discover complete silence with regard to both. There are no
letters between April 9th and June 18th; no journaling from
May 14th to June 26th. Something very unusual must have
been occurring. Toward the end of June, Teilhard names
certain elements of the interior crisis he had just undergone.[5]

A first aspect he calls a "sort of numbness" regarding his
military responsibilities. He notes in his *Journal*:

I've been very depressed of late. I can't muster any effort
. . . My natural energies have been depleted. I'm near
exhaustion.

To Marguerite he confesses:

I no longer feel like myself — the individual monad so
full of plans for personal activity. Rather I feel lost in this
gigantic clash of nations and brutal energies. I am left
drained and depersonalized.

4. "The Heart of Matter" (1950), in *HM*, pp. 26-28.
5. The following quotations are taken from his *Journal* (June 26-30) and from a letter (June
18) to Marguerite in *MM*, pp. 100-101.

A second dimension of the trial is his experience of Christ. During those long periods on the front, he was prevented from celebrating Mass: "How distant Our Lord seems to me now!"

Teilhard indicates two other characteristics of his crisis in this prayer which he addresses to Jesus:

> My soul is weighed down and anxious. My mind and heart are captivated by ideals which I sometimes fear may be neither heavenly enough nor sufficiently orthodox. O Master, preserve in me and in those whom I love so much — whatever the cost! — the light of your purity and your truth.

By naming "heart" and "purity" Teilhard is referring to his vow of celibacy. A glance at his *Journal* earlier in the year reveals how preoccupied he was with sexuality and chastity: February 8, 10, 14, 20; March 9, 14; April 27, 29; May 3-6, 8-10 (1916). He was struggling intensely to integrate his love for a particular woman with his commitment to Christ.

Teilhard's prayer concerning his "mind" and "truth" is in reference to the mounting conflict within him occasioned by cries of unorthodoxy coming from some confreres. Those suspicions clashed directly with what he considered a personal charism — the reconciliation of God and the World. "My vocation is to be the apostle of Communion with God through the Cosmos."[6]

Teilhard reveals yet another aspect of the crisis of May-June 1916:

> What has been going on in me this month is a loss of my will to live. The very source of my energy has gone out of me. "If salt becomes insipid, how can it be made salty again?" [Mt 5:13]. I seem to have lost all confidence and interest in myself.

In that frame of mind, Teilhard asks himself what should be his interior attitude:

6. *Journal*, 22 Dec. 1917.

What is one to do when one can find no support of any kind? I must hold fast to Our Lord without feeling anything, and pray . . . For if I succeed in doing that, what joy and peace I will discover in humbling myself without limit before Christ. In losing myself in him, I let go all confidence in myself . . . until I am completely united with his divine will!

On the feast of the Sacred Heart (June 30, 1916), Teilhard synthesized the various elements of his trial as well as their profound import:

I can see more clearly now what was so disconcerting at Verdun. It was the concrete and immediate probability of being killed on the battlefield. . . . I experienced in every fiber of my being what it means to be utterly lost and to have to abandon every cherished hope, every meaningful plan. . . . That threat overshadowed me . . . freezing all my ardor. My will to live and to act was wiped out. . . . The very sources of my life dried up . . . The heart of Our Lord remains the font of all the passivities which exert mastery over me and of all the activities which awaken me and propel me forward.

The events of May-June 1916 are among the most significant in the interior genesis of Teilhard de Chardin. Before attaining that breakthrough, he underwent a long and painstaking maturation under God's guidance. This spiritual threshold constitutes for him a radical personal conversion, a true spiritual death and resurrection. It was as if the old Teilhard had died somewhere in the fierce fighting around Verdun in order to allow the new Teilhard to be reborn out of the depths of human despair.[7]

D. *Promoting the Passivities of Existence*

What must be not only our attitude towards, but also our

7. See "Christ in Matter" (1916), in *HU*, pp. 41-55 and in *HM*, pp. 61-67.

voluntary collaboration with, all that we undergo throughout life? Teilhard responds:

> I do not give way passively to these blessed passivities, Lord. Rather I offer myself actively to them, and I do all in my power to promote them.[8]

To offer ourselves to the passivities of existence means to be open to them, to leave ourselves open before them, and above all to let ourselves be opened by them. It denotes persisting in an attitude of Christian resignation which invites and fosters the presence in us of a Power-greater-than-ourselves.

That resignation is not inertly passive. It is active in two senses: (1) Together with God, we energetically resist evil. (2) Abandonment to God is itself an affirmative act. We say "yes" to those passivities and honestly mean it. Therefore, if we are to commune in depth with God operating within us and all around us, it is not enough to simply let come what may. We must positively give ourselves to him who comes in and through the very act of receiving.

Nonetheless, that positive resignation, as extensive and comprehensive as it may be, still does not exhaust all the richness of our collaboration with Christ. The complete offering of self to God attains its fullness only when accompanied by maximum personal effort to produce the best possible *ópus* (work, labor, task, product). In the faithful accomplishment of our daily responsibilities — even down to the most minute details — we bring Christ a little more fulfillment. Thus, we not only make up for what is lacking in the passion of Christ (Col 1:24), but we also contribute our share in making up what is lacking in his action.

By both our passivities and our activities, then, we do our best qualitatively and quantitatively to promote as fully as possible the creative, formative action of God within us and around us. In that twofold way, we contribute positively to the

8. "The Priest" (1918), in *Writings*, p. 215.

transformation of all things through him, with him and in him. For in whatever we suffer, undergo, endure, we receive Christ. And in whatever we do, foster, improve — not only in terms of good intention (*operátio*), but also in the material aspect of the activity (*ópus*) — we collaborate with Christ in building up his Body (Ep 4:16).

Teilhard sees activity as related to the passivities of existence in four complementary ways.[9]

First, the power to act is itself received in the primordial gift of existence: "What do you have that you have not received?" (1 Cor 4:7). That very "first fruit of the Spirit" (Rm 8:23) for each person is his/her gift of being-becoming.

Second, maximum effort and maximum fidelity in every undertaking serve as essential signs authenticating evangelical receptivity. That effort prunes and discerns the passivities of existence from inert passivity, laziness and the temptation of matter.

Third, the daily accomplishment of one's responsibilities with uncompromising fidelity constitutes a formidable asceticism. Detachment through action! If I really do minute-by-minute, hour-by-hour all that God's providence asks of me through the converging circumstances of the moment, then the Lord will purge me of self-centeredness through my fidelity to that activity.

Fourth, an active and vigorous resistance against all evil is necessary in order to arrive at true Christian resignation.

Our considerations in these last two chapters have focused on the passivities of existence, of life, of living, of being, of becoming. After World War I, however, Teilhard ceases using the expression *les passivités de l'existence* in preference for a more precise designation based on the way they strike the person undergoing them. Henceforth, he distinguishes passivities of growth and passivities of diminishment.

---

9. See *DM*, pp. 49-73, 90-93.

CHAPTER 14

PASSIVITIES OF GROWTH
AND OF DIMINISHMENT

Pierre Teilhard de Chardin composed his first full-length book
— *The Divine Milieu* (1927) — as a testimony to his deepest
convictions regarding the spiritual life. That book comprises
three sections: (1) the divinization of our activities, (2) the
divinization of our passivities and (3) the Divine Milieu proper.
The passivities of growth and of diminishment are the subject
of the second section of his book as well as the focus of the next
two chapters of our work. [1]

Teilhard dedicated *The Divine Milieu* to "those who love
the World," since "God so loved the World" (Jn 3:16). One
common trait among addicted, codependent and attached
persons is a lack of concern for the World. With their desire
fixated on some mood-alteration, they use the world for all that
they can get out of it. Thus, essential to recovery is learning
how to give of oneself to God and to others in and through the
World. Our activities provide one means of moving in that
direction. Our passivities afford another context in which the
gift of self contributes to a better World — hence, to God's
reign.

The divinization of our passivities of growth lead us to
new depths and meaning in our encounter with the Power-

1. All quotations in this chapter, unless otherwise identified, are found in *DM*, pp. 11,
74-83.

greater-than-ourselves. The divinization of our passivities of diminishment furnish us new insight into the positive and constructive potential inherent in human suffering.

A. *The Rhythm of Growing and Diminishing*

After a lengthy development of our powers, energies and capacities, we eventually begin to acknowledge the influence of passivities in our lives. Little by little, we become conscious that we receive immeasurably more than we give. We gradually recognize that we are dominated by the objects of our conquests:

> Like Jacob wrestling with his nocturnal Messenger [Gn 32:26-31], the soul faithful to life and to grace ends up adoring the One against whom it was struggling.

That is to say:

> [Paradoxically], the soul has hardly arrived at the heart of things, when it finds itself ready to be detached from them. Having taken its fill of the Universe and of itself, the soul one day discovers that it is possessed by an intense need to die to self and to be led beyond itself. Moreover, this is not the effect of disillusionment, but rather results from a logical development of its own effort. [2]

That truth is but a restatement of the baptismal symbol: namely, that immersion in the World with Christ — the first phase of our incorporation in him — is followed by emergence through the World with him. To paraphrase John the Baptizer: Initially, I must increase so that Christ may increase. Eventually, however, I must decrease so that he can further increase (cf. Jn 3:30).

2. "Forma Christi" (1918), in *Writings*, p. 261. See *Contemplation*, pp. 117-122; *Spiritual Journey*, pp. 41, 45-50, 55-74, 99-113.

Immersion and emergence are like breathing in and breathing out; like the arsis and thesis of a musical measure. The more we take in, the more we let out and let go; the greater the upbeat, the more meaningful the downbeat. Thus, the more realistic our involvement in creation for Christ, the more complete our detachment from creatures with him. These are not two movements, but the same movement in two phases. Each phase is characterized by its own type of receptivity. The passivities of growth pertain mainly to the sphere of immersion, while the passivities of diminishment are associated principally with emergence. As a matter of fact, our activities are sandwiched between those two genres of passivities. We receive the ability to act. We then activate that capacity, which activity leads us ultimately to abandonment to God in love.

In its most general sense, therefore, the term "passivities" refers to everything that is received by and within the human person. What is not done by us is by definition undergone in us. Thus, our passivities embrace the immense complex of everything within us and all around us, without us and in spite of us. That complex is as vast, as intricate and as incomprehensible as the totality of the World's past and present.

From the point of view of receiving those passivities, we distinguish two groups. This distinction stems from the surface perception of them as being amicable or painful to us. Those friendly and favorable forces that sustain our effort and point the way toward what we ordinarily consider success, we call *passivities of growth.* Those hostile powers which obstruct our innate tendencies, hampering what we generally consider progress toward heightened being we term *passivities of diminishment.*

B. *Passivities of Growth*

We undergo Life at least as much as,
if not more than, we undergo Death.

That truth eventually impresses itself upon the consciousness of every reflective person. Living and dying. Are
they something we do, or are they done to us? In their deepest
sense, both life and death are actively received in us, by us.
They happen to us. Therefore, they are primarily passive. Yet
there is also something we must do with respect to each of
them. In the case of life, we have to correspond to it, cooperate
with it. If not, the gift is squandered. In the case of death, we
must accept it, become resigned to God through it and beyond
it. Not only do we have to say *amén*, but we must especially be
amén. Regarding both life and death the prayer of recovery
from addiction, codependency and attachment is applicable:

> God grant me
> > the serenity to accept the things I cannot change,
> > the courage to change (improve) the things I can, and
> > the wisdom to know the difference.

Living and growing are so natural to us that we rarely
pause long enough to distinguish our activities from the host of
passivities which nourish them. We generally take for granted
our health, our self, our life, until something happens — an
illness, a contradiction, a death.

How then do we get in touch with that immense wealth of
reality which Teilhard calls our passivities of growth? What do
they consist in? Concretely, what are they?

We must penetrate prayerfully the elusive depths of our
inner selves and there try to perceive the ocean of forces to
which we are subjected and in which our personal as well as
collective development is steeped. We have to enter into
ourselves in deepest recollection to imbibe the profundity and
universality of our dependence on so much which remains
altogether outside our control and which goes to make up the
intimacy of our communion with the World to which we belong.

Therefore, with the light of faith and intuition, I leave
behind the zone of everyday preoccupations and relationships
where everything has a name, a place and a number, to search

and to listen with my heart to those regions whence I feel dimly that my power to act emanates. Yet, as I move further and further away from the conventional certainties on which social life thrives, I discover that I am losing contact with my usual self. At each step of the descent a new aspect of personhood is disclosed within me, the name of which I am no longer certain and which no longer obeys me. Moreover, when I stop my exploration because the path fades from beneath my steps, I find a fathomless abyss at my feet, out of which comes — I know not whence — the stream which I dare call *my* life.

My life. *Víta méa!* My life is not really mine (*méi*) as if it were *of* me. Rather it is *to* me (*míhi*). For what is mine that I have not received (1 Cor 4:7)? And what have I received that is not destined by God for transformation (Rm 8:29-30)?

Will any human knowledge be able to reveal to me the unfathomable origins of my being? I may be able to trace my roots back a few generations. By means of certain disciplines, I might even stabilize or enlarge some aspects of my ability to receive. Yet no discipline can harness the deepest sources of life. Neither I nor anyone else can effectively change who I am and who I am becoming:

> My self is given to me far more than it is formed by me. In the ultimate analysis the interior life, life at its source, the nascent life completely eludes my grasp.

That is the *first* fruit of my interior journey to discover the passivities of growth.

The *second* flows from the first. Terrified by that realization, something in me wants to return to the light of day and forget this disturbing enigma in comfortable settings and familiar surroundings. This temptation of matter would have me forsake my salutary quest and settle instead for lassitude, complacency and mediocrity. Yet just when I am about to succumb, there — beyond the darkness and confusion — appears the Unknown, the I-don't-know-what, the Power-greater-than-myself that I am trying to escape. It (s/he) is not only deeper than the abyss, but also intimately intertwined among the innumerable strands of the web of providence. It (s/he) is the very stuff of which the universe and my own individuality are woven. It (s/he) infinitely transcends my life and my world, yet remains the immanent, vital force not only at the Alpha and Omega of my being, but also all the way through my becoming.

A *third* effect also results from my interior journey to search out the passivities of growth. I begin to reel even more when I contemplate — much less try to number — the myriad of favorable influences which must have converged to produce me. I could go out of my mind analyzing the supreme improbability, the incalculable unlikelihood of finding myself existing at all in a world that has actually survived and succeeded in being a world. Thus, having come to the realization that my life is not really mine, but has been given to me, and that I am called infinitely beyond myself, I discover the indescribable poverty of my spirit and the ultimate meaning of the first Beatitude:

> Blessed are those who know their true need,
> for God is theirs and they are God's (Mt 5:3).

Or. to rephrase that Beatitude in terms of the first and second principles of the Twelve-Step Program:

> Blessed are those who admit their powerlessness over addictions, codependency and attachments, and acknowledge that their lives have become unmanageable.
> For now they can begin to be receptive to a Power-greater-than-themselves.

There is still a *fourth* dimension to my inner quest. The fourth recapitulates the previous three. As anyone who dares to make the pilgrimage will find, I feel the anxiety characteristic of a person lost, adrift, floundering, when I encounter the fathomlessness of my own personhood, the utter transcendency of the God for whom my soul pines and the seeming endlessness of my inner poverty. If something — or Someone — saved me from my distress, it was the gentle and unmistakable voice of Jesus coming across the lake and out of the depths of the night:

> I am.
> Be not afraid (Jn 6:20).

More realistic faith in the Son of God is the culminating effect of the Christian quest to encounter the passivities of growth.

That faith, however, must be actualized in daily life, in attitudes and action. In the Life that wells up in me (Jn 4:14) and in the Matter which sustains me, I find much more than God's gift. I encounter the Lord himself — he who makes me participate in his being and molds me in his likeness (2 Cor 3:18). I discover the two hands, as it were, of the Father. One hand holds me so firmly, yet so tenderly, that it coincides with all the sources of my life. In it, I experience God's immanence. The other hand stretches beyond my wildest imagination in all-embracing harmony, holding together the immensity of the cosmos. In it, I encounter his transcendence.

I respond to that discovery two ways: (1) by my personal will to be and to become in a more qualitative fashion; (2) by making my contribution to the being and ultimate becoming of all the created realities which providence affords me. In other words, I am careful never to stifle, distort or waste my power to love, to do or to become. Furthermore, I strive never to miss an opportunity to direct others toward Spirit.

C. Passivities of Diminishment

To be open to a Power-greater-than-ourselves within the internal and external forces which animate our being and sustain its development means basically to receive and to trust all the influences of life. In responding to the passivities of growth by our fidelity to action, we commune with God. Thus, the desire to undergo the Lord leads us to the satisfying task of promoting our own advancement and that of others. However:

> The soul faithful to Life and to Grace cannot proceed indefinitely in the direction of building up a strong self . . . It gradually becomes aware of the emergence from the very operation of its impulse toward self-fulfillment of another component which grows more dominant — the predilection for detachment.[3]

How amazing! The zest for being and the quest for wholeness have within their inner dynamics the predilection for detachment and ultimately for death. Moreover, that development is the logical and necessary outcome of Progress toward Spirit. All true growth, all real maturation is accomplished finally only through a *metánoia*:

> The World cannot attain consummate fulfillment except through a death, a "night" . . . The Earth does not take cognizance of its destiny except through the crisis of a conversion.[4]

To encounter God as the animator of the passivities of growth is awesome. It is terrifying, freeing and hope-imbued all at the same time. Yet what is this predilection for detachment? We can understand something of the meaning of gusto for life, of zest for being and becoming. But how can anyone develop a taste for detachment? The fact that a Power-greater-than-ourselves is discovered in and through life we readily accept. Yet can God be found not only also, but above all, in and through death? The incontestable lesson of every living creature and of all interior progress has always been that one must die in order to rise transformed:

> Unless the grain of wheat falls into the ground and dies,
> it remains only a seed (Jn 12:24).

3. "Forma Christi" (1918), in *Writings*, p. 260.
4. *Cor*. p. 31; "The Spirit of the Earth" (1931), in *HE*, p. 38.

> Whoever finds his/her life will lose it,
>> and whoever loses his/her life for my sake will find it
>> (Mt 10:39).

Resurrection not only follows death, in the sense of coming after the dying process, but resurrection occurs especially in death, through it and out of it.

The passivities of growth develop us. These friendly and favorable forces which sustain our effort and direct us toward Progress perceptibly foster advancement. Nevertheless, in an extremely paradoxical manner the passivities of diminishment cause us to mature even more. These hostile powers which in one way reduce and even destroy our capacities for development constitute in another sphere the passivities par excellence by which we commune with God:

> Although outwardly we are falling into decay,
>> inwardly we are being transformed day-by-day
>> (2 Cor 4:16).

Of all that we undergo in this earthly sojourn, the passivities of diminishment remain those most charged with power to divinize.

The expressions "of growth" and "of diminishment" designate, then, a division of the passivities of existence into two general categories. Those qualifying words denote that aspect which at first sight strikes the observer. Some passivities appear friendly, others hostile. However, beyond their appearances both genres exercise a positive and interacting influence on our spiritualization.

How is that possible? The response of Teilhard is that of St. Paul:

> For those who love God,
>> everything is transformed into good (Rm 8:28).

And they do mean absolutely everything (cf. Rm 8:31-39).

The forces of diminishment are, nonetheless, our passivities in the fullest sense. Not only do we suffer them, but also we suffer immensely from them. The ways that they affect us are innumerable. Their forms are infinitely varied. Their influence is constant. We can divide them into two groups: those diminishments which originate within us and those which assail us from the outside.

Generally speaking, the external passivities of diminishment comprise our experiences of ill fortune. They spring up from all sides. They are the microbe which infects the body or the inopportune word that wounds the heart. They are the incidents and the accidents of varying importance and diverse kinds which crush us, hurt us, anger and frustrate us. They are the barriers that block our way, the walls that hem us in, the defeats that bring us down.

All those passivities are diminishing enough. Yet the ones whose origin is within us "comprise the darkest element and the most despairingly useless years of our lives." They are all the physical, intellectual and moral limitations that plague us, restrict us, humiliate us from birth to death. They are the temperamental, nervous, personality and emotional disorders which constantly nag us. They are our moodiness, our woundedness, our innumerable manifestations of selfishness. Even the passage of time is a formidable passivity. It is either too long or too short, too cluttered or too empty, too much or not enough. In the end, old age itself gradually robs us of all vigor, pushing us irreversibly toward death.

Death. "Death is the apex and the consummation of all our diminishments. Death is the epitome of all evil." It epitomizes physical evil inasmuch as it results organically from the complete disintegration of the matter to which we are subject. It epitomizes moral evil inasmuch as it is immeasurably compounded by the abuse of freedom and by the sin of the world (Jn 1:29). Yet death surrenders us totally to God. Through it, we pass over completely to Someone-greater-than-ourselves.

Thus death is also supreme good. But how? How can that which is the epitome of evil be transformed into the greatest good? The next chapter formulates a faith response.

CHAPTER 15

DEALING WITH OUR PASSIVITIES OF DIMINISHMENT

One of the greatest difficulties that addicted, codependent or attached persons experience in persevering in recovery is dealing with the intense pain which accompanies the process. In the throes of suffering, people tend to lose sight of its potential for interior growth. Some faith-imbued understanding of how God uses diminishment for our good does, however, help us undergo that pain in a spirit of authentic Christian resignation. This chapter synthesizes how Pierre Teilhard de Chardin sees a Power-greater-than-ourselves converting evil into good — how the Lord transforms us in himself through adversity.[1]

A. *The Struggle With God Against Evil*

The first question we must pose regarding the transformation of evil into good is this: What is the relationship of God to evil? For our purposes, we summarize three points of view. They are that of (1) the Medieval scholastics, (2) St. John of the Cross and (3) Teilhard de Chardin.

(1) The classical scholastic outlook is formulated according to these distinctions: God wills good directly. The Lord

---

1. All quotations in this chapter, unless otherwise identified are found in *DM*, pp. 83-93.

wills physical evil only indirectly. God merely permits moral evil.

(2) The Sanjuanist perspective introduces into that tripartite framework certain subtle nuances. Even during the most trying agonies of the night of sense, the influence of God within us remains constant and positive. In fact, it is the Lord's loving, transforming activity in direct contact with our inner poverty that produces all the pain and darkness which John calls night. God himself "sends" these storms and trials so that we may advance more securely in our search for absolute good.[2] These storms exercise us, disposing and accommodating our senses for union with God in love. Even Jesus "was led by the Spirit into the desert in order to be tempted" (Mt 4:1).

(3) Teilhard adds a complementary insight to the two preceding views. When suffering befalls him/her, the Christian prays with Job (19:21), "The Lord has touched me." That statement is, of course, profoundly true. Yet that affirmation, so tersely formulated, also summarizes a long development and a complex of influences — some very good and joyful, others very evil and painful. Thus, only when we have passed all the way through these influences, do those words reach their full import.

If we go back to the beginning of our encounters with painful situations, we realize that we prayed at the outset — and continued thereafter — as did Jesus in Gethsemane: Lord, free me from this diminishment. I want with all my being to assist you in removing this chalice from me. However, not my will, but yours be done (cf. Lk 22:41-44).

Those words express the first will, so to speak, of our Father: namely, that every evil — especially physical, emotional and mental suffering — be reduced to a minimum. Indeed, he wills that it be entirely eliminated whenever possible. The Father wishes each of us to struggle together with him against all evil. Therefore, at the approach of diminishments, we are called to utilize all our resources in order to struggle against whatever is of evil in them. That resistance is abso-

2. See Chapter 9 of this book: C. Causes of Purgation.

lutely necessary if we are to adhere as faithfully as possible to the creative action of God within us and around us.

However, even if we wrestle with God against evil, despite every effort we shall sooner or later be vanquished by evil. For in the end, each person must die. How then do we find God's will in that? What is the significance of inevitable defeat?

B. Our Apparent Defeat and Its Transformation

The problem of evil — that is, the reconciliation of our failures with God's creative goodness and power — remains for both our hearts and minds one of the most disturbing mysteries of the universe. It is all the more perplexing when we read in the Gospel "that it is necessary for scandal to occur" (Mt 18:7). To admit that failure, sin and death do exist is difficult enough. But what is even more troubling to acknowledge is that they *must* be.

(1) Why Must Pain Exist?

Teilhard offers several ways which afford some understanding in faith of that enigma. Each response focuses on God's providence in the actual economy of salvation. Teilhard does not speculate on "what-if's" or "what-might-have-been's."

A *first* response stems from two aspects of the evolutionary process itself. (A) Everything that becomes naturally suffers and commits its own faults. Of the three phases of the dialectic of evolution — divergence, convergence, emergence — a person cannot get through the initial one without experiencing many blind alleys, dead-ends and explorations incompatible with self-fulfillment. In the ultimate analysis, each of us learns and grows by experience. Moreover, that experience is gained only at the price of much pain and hurt, many mistakes and failures. (B) In every aspect of evolution, there is both continuity and discontinuity. In the process of becoming, something endures and something is necessarily left behind. Nature abounds with examples: the grain of wheat, the caterpillar, the cutting of the apron strings, etc. All that detachment entails intense suffering.

A *second* response flows from the nature of evolution, especially as directed toward a point of ultimate consummation. Evolution — or more precisely "genesis" — denotes movement from incompleteness to wholeness. It is transition from scatteredness to unification, passage from chaos to accomplished being. That movement necessitates fierce struggle, both interior and exterior. One cannot succeed in becoming more without exerting immense effort at considerable cost of energy. We have only to think of the discipline exerted by athletes, scholars and diplomats.

A *third* response views the laws of statistical necessity latent within evolution. The universe contains such a multitude of agents pursuing their individual and collective progress that some of those energies are bound not only to cross paths but also to clash head-on. Many cycles of nature are predicated upon the following principle: What is good for one individual may mean death for another. What is food for the fox is end for the rabbit. In that vein, plants drain minerals from the soil, cattle eat the plants, humans dine on beef, and then fertilize the ground. Other examples related to the laws of statistical necessity can be given: traffic fatality predictions for the Labor Day weekend, Murphy's Law ("Whatever can go wrong sooner or later will").

A *fourth* response considers the inner nature of created being becoming. Within creation as a whole and within each monad, there exist two contrary forces: entropy and evolution. Entropy is that innate tendency which turns the creature in upon itself. Evolution — especially in the Teilhardian sense of genesis — is that energy within each being driving it beyond its present state to actualize its full potential. Translated into the human sphere, entropy produces self-centeredness, pride, woundedness. Evolution, on the other hand, elicits gift of self, commitment, love.

When we understand the above four responses in the light of Christ, the necessity of suffering and death assumes a new significance and a decidedly positive thrust. Not only are we called to become fully human, but also to participate in God's own life — to be transformed in God. Thus:

> If being united means in every case passing on and dying at least partially in/to what one loves, then detachment . . . must be all the more complete the more we give our attachment to the One-who-is-greater-than-ourselves. We can set no limits to the uprooting that is involved on our journey in God.

(2) *Why Didn't God Make a Better World?*

The above responses offer much food for reflection. Yet the myopic person still counters: Couldn't God have made a better world? A universe without pain, failure, death? A journey that would be easier, simpler, more enjoyable? That narcissistic view of creation perceives the cost of progress as good or bad inasmuch as it suits or does not suit one's likes and dislikes.

Even transcending a self-centered appraisal of divine providence, we see God's day-to-day caring for us only upside down and in reverse — as if viewing the underneath portion of a tapestry. At best, all we observe are loose ends and disjointed patterns. Instead, we must regard the world and our life in faith from God's loving perspective — looking at the tapestry from right side up, as it were. For God did indeed make the best possible world according to his purpose, which is transforming union.

Thus our defeat only appears to be defeat. We merely seem to fail. In view of Jesus's paschal mystery, no effort is wasted, no struggle is in vain, no death is without some victory (1 Cor 15:54-55). Everything is transformed into good for those who believe in him (Rm 8:28). That good may not, however, be apparent to the victim: for example, to the soldier who falls during the assault which leads to peace. Nevertheless, God does bring forth not only some good but specifically a greater good. The Lord produces something greater than what would otherwise have been:

> Like the artist who knows how to use a flaw in the rock s/he sculpts in order to bring out more exquisite lines, God — provided that we abandon ourselves to him in faith and love — transforms everything into our good. For those who seek the Lord, not everything is immediately good, but everything is capable of becoming good.

And, we might add: not only *good* or even *better*, but absolutely the *best*, since the goal of it all is transforming union with God.

(3) *How God Converts Evil into Good*

Providence can be said to convert evil into good in three general ways.

The *first* is after the manner of Job. A defeat diverts our energies toward more propitious endeavors, but on the same level of human means and ends: for example, the merchant who loses his/her business in a fire. That misfortune forces the person to start the same business all over again, but this time s/he becomes even more prosperous than before.

The *second* way occurs when a fall, a setback or a failure diverts our energies toward more spiritual pursuits. These are the many *felix culpas* which dot our existence: the knife that prunes, the sin which brings us to our senses, the accident that radically changes the course of our life. The misfortune forces us to more qualitative levels of activity and receptivity.

In each of those two modes, providence allows us to see some concrete results of our suffering. We can say that at least eventually we come to understand something of why our defeat happened at all or why it occurred under certain circumstances. Our minds and hearts are at least partially at rest, for now we see a reason. We are somewhat satisfied. It was a blessing in disguise, a happy chance, a paradoxical grace.

However, the *third* way providence converts evil into good leaves us completely in the dark. It concerns the far more common and much more difficult situations in which our understanding remains totally frustrated. These are the situations where we can see no good whatsoever coming out of evil. These are the instances where no profit can be perceived on any material or spiritual level to counterbalance the diminishment: a crib death, an irreconcilable divorce, ravaging famines, suppression of human rights by brute force, genocide, etc. Yet, "this is the most efficacious and the most sanctifying way of all ways."

C. Communion with God in Faith Through Diminishment

The Christian response to the above dilemma, according to Teilhard, is communion with God in extremely dark faith through the diminishment which we are undergoing. How then does he understand with respect to our spiritual journey the providential contribution of faith and of death which is the epitome of all diminishments?

(1) The Darkness of Faith and Death

Specifically regarding the obscurity of faith, Teilhard observes:

> I, as much as anyone, walk in the darkness of faith . . . In order to account for that darkness which is so contradictory to divine light, some spiritual masters try to explain that the Lord intentionally hides himself from us to test our love. One would have to be irretrievably lost in mental gymnastics or utterly insensitive to the agonizing doubts within oneself and others not to perceive the inveterate inhumanness of such a solution . . . To my mind, that darkness is simply a specific instance of the problem of evil . . . If the Lord allows us to suffer, to sin

and to doubt, it is because he cannot immediately and in one fell swoop heal us and manifest himself completely to us. Moreover, if God cannot, it is solely because we are still incapable of letting him do it, since we have not yet passed beyond our pilgrim state.[3]

Concerning the mystery of death, Teilhard considers every diminishment a kind of death. Death, properly speaking, is the definitive detachment of the human person from every experiential point of reference; that is, from every perceptible or tangible framework in this life. Each detachment is a severance from some point of reference in this mortal world. All daily deaths are recapitulated and consummated in the end by personal death. Thus, for all of us living in faith (Gal 2:20), death becomes the only way capable of definitively detaching and wrenching us from all in us that is not transformable in God.

Yet, in order that faith be unconditional abandonment to ineffable love, complete darkness in relation to every experiential framework is necessary. Otherwise, we will not let go. We will irresistibly hang on for dear life.

However, only our loving Father, who knows exactly what we need in proper measure, can prune us in such a way as to preserve in us all that is transformable in himself, while cutting away all that is incapable of becoming divinized (Jn 15:1-5).

Teilhard expresses the intensity and all-embraciveness of our abandonment in darkest faith to God through the symbol of the *órans* — or, more precisely, of the *ádorans*:

> To adore. That means to become lost in the Unfathomable, to plunge into the Inexhaustible, to find peace in the Incorruptible . . . It is to offer oneself to the [all-consuming and transforming] Fire of divine love, to let oneself consciously and voluntarily be annihilated in the measure that one becomes aware [of one's inner poverty].

---

3. "How I Believe" (1934), in *CE*, pp. 131-132.

To adore means to give of one's deepest to One whose depth has no end . . . To adore is to lose oneself unitively in God.[4]

(2) *Why Total Darkness?*

The question still remains, however: Why can unreserved surrender in faith to God be accomplished only in total darkness?

A first response stems from the overpowering nature of faith as divine light. Because we are still immersed in the limitations of this mortal existence, that light — which of itself is so pure and illuminating — has an obscuring effect on our powers of comprehension. Only the complete detachment wrought by death can definitively break through those limitations.

Another response arises from the paradoxically positive role that darkness plays in the intensification of abandonment in faith. Darkness does not cause faith or an increase in faith. God alone is its cause, together with our voluntary cooperation. However, darkness is the necessary condition for an increase in faith. The more we walk in darkness, the more we are providentially disposed toward surrender. When darkness is total, abandonment to the Power-greater-than-ourselves is perfect. That is, in essence, what death so effectively accomplishes. It is precisely the situation of complete darkness in death which allows us to pass into total Light.

Everything which bespeaks life in us spontaneously abhors darkness and letting go. We instinctively reach out for some support, some crutch. If allowed to have its way, that aspect of our humanness would lead irresistibly to attachment, if not also to addiction and codependency. It is necessary, therefore, that every support be removed, ultimately even that of this earthly existence. That detaching is the principal effect of the darkness of faith. It eliminates progressively all the supports to which we innately cling. In the end — in death —

4. *DM*, pp. 127-128; "The Evolution of Chastity" (1934), in *TF*, p. 65.

that darkness removes even the possibility of clinging to anything by forming the concrete milieu in which we have no one
and nothing to depend on except a Power-greater-than-
ourselves.

At the outset of our faith journey, God leaves to us much
of the initiative in our purification. Through self-knowledge,
we perceive certain attachments. We then take specific mea-
sures to remove those obstacles so as to continue our passage
through creation. We detach ourselves to the degree we can.
Gradually, however, as we perceive the limitations of our
efforts and the preponderant efficacy of God's activity within
us, that initiative is transformed into abandonment to him. God
uses the passivities of existence to actualize our potential. Yet
of all those passivities, those of diminishment are the most
sanctifying since they are also the most detaching. In their
darkness, they favor most efficaciously the full development of
surrender in faith.

God, however, does not directly darken the soul. The
Lord takes no pleasure in pain or death. Rather, he unites us to
himself and divinizes us, but in a manner which respects
completely the laws of mortal being. God permits the normal
activity of the interior and exterior forces of growth and diminishment to ascend toward definitive metamorphosis. These
diminishments in themselves represent the destruction of being. However, through them and beyond the darkness which
they cause, we encounter God in faith and love.

(3) *Evil's Defeat*

Communion with God through death coincides then with
his· victory (and ours in him) over evil. Nonetheless, true
victory over evil is situated in the realm of faith, beyond evil
itself. Evil as such is not directly destroyed. It does not have to
be. For, left to itself as we transcend it by faith, evil self-
destructs, falling back by its own weight into the multiple —
that is, into what Matthew calls "exterior darkness" (Mt 8:12;
22:13; 25:30). That movement occurs in and through the

personal death of each individual. It will happen collectively at the end of the world.

The dying Christ conquered evil not by destroying it directly, but rather by not letting it destroy him, even though it literally killed him. Jesus allowed evil to destroy itself in trying to destroy him. (Deicide is the absolute epitome of all conceivable and actual evil.) In his death, Christ passed through evil to the Father. In death, by his interior act of total submission to the Father as well as by his theandric love for him and for creation, Jesus allowed his divinity to permeate completely his humanity. Thus, he transformed it in God and detached it from all the limitations of this mortal existence. Yes, Christ resisted evil right up to the end in that he did not allow it to vanquish him interiorly. Jesus's submission was to the Father alone. He never capitulated to evil. So too for us in him. By abandonment in faith, we rise with Christ above and beyond every death, leaving evil behind in outer darkness.

Thus, the agonizing Christian prays:

> It is not enough, Lord, to die while communing with you.
> Teach me to commune in the very act of dying.

Not only does increasing communion with God eventually lead us to pass from this life, but also in faith we experience communion with the Power-greater-than-ourselves through the darkness of the act of dying.

D. True Christian Resignation

For Teilhard, our attitude toward diminishments comprises two essential elements: (1) maximum effort against whatever is of evil in them and (2) optimum receptivity to God alone through them and beyond them. That combination constitutes active submission to the Father's will, whether we are speaking of the obedience of Jesus to the Father or of our own obedience to him in Christ. Resignation is truly Christian only inasmuch as we make a vigorous resistance with God against evil. That resistance arises from our unlimited abandonment to and trust in God beyond evil.

When we miss doing all in our power to resist a given evil, we find ourselves lacking the quality of receptivity willed by God. Consequently, we cannot undergo him as much as we could have otherwise. When our effort is courageous and persevering, we encounter God through the evil, beyond the evil. In that way, "the optimum of our communion in resignation indeed coincides with the maximum of our fidelity to human effort."

However, we must not conceive of that effort against evil and that receptivity to God in succession, as if one follows the other. Both coexist from the beginning and endure to the end. On the one hand, maximum effort safeguards receptivity so that it does not become capitulation to evil rather than submission to God beyond evil. On the other hand, abandonment to God ensures that the effort in question is not against God but solely against evil.

Christian resignation is not something residual, as if it were merely the consequence of all else having failed. Christian resignation is inherently positive, because it is toward God. We are not resigned, properly speaking, either to suffering or to death. We are resigned only to God, deeper than the pain and beyond the dying. We must resist all suffering and death with every ounce of our strength. Then, when exterior resistance is no longer possible, like Christ's our interior resistance must continue up to the end. The final human act of each one of us in faith is toward Life beyond death.

True Christian resignation emerges, therefore, at the point of convergence between the struggle against evil and our receptivity to God alone. It is the point where God exercises his full primacy over us as we abandon ourselves to him.

Having resisted evil for God with all our force, we arrive sooner or later at inevitable defeat — defeat, that is, according to our experiential framework. That is the hour par excellence of Christian resignation:

[For if we accept diminishment in faith] without ceasing to struggle against it, the diminishment itself can become for us a loving source of renewal . . . In the realm of faith, a further dimension exists which allows God to effect imperceptibly a mysterious reversal of evil into good. Leaving behind the zone of human successes and failures, the Christian reaches by trust in the One-greater-than-him/herself the region of suprasensible transformations and growths. In this way, resignation is the energy which transposes the field of his/her activity into a higher realm.

Thus death is not only *le Mal*, but it coincides in a transcendent manner with the recapitulation and consummation of Christian resignation. Death is the apex of communion with God in darkest faith. It is the loss of self in One-greater-than-self. Death becomes the place of limitless abandonment to God in himself.

CHAPTER 16

RECEPTIVITY OF A SUPERIOR ORDER IN RELATION TO SPIRITUALIZATION

In *The Mystical Milieu* (1917), Pierre Teilhard de Chardin refers to a certain receptivity of a superior order:

> In their eagerness to promote the reign of God, there was a time when searchers found themselves intensely involved in activity. Now, however, the process is reversed. The very exuberance of their zest for action leads them in the direction of *une passivité d'ordre supérieur.*[1]

When referring to the passivities of existence, which he later qualifies with the phrases "of growth" and "of diminishment," Teilhard consistently employs the plural: *les passivités.* In the context of "a superior order," however, *passivité* occurs in the singular. The reason for the change seems to be this: In the latter case, he is not designating a host of influences. Instead, he is stressing a basic interior stance: that of remaining receptive to the influence of a Power-greater-than-ourselves within us and around us in a variety of situations. Thus it is a question of our fundamental stance toward all passivities — whether of existence, of growth or of diminishment. That receptive attitude increases as God brings us into the more advanced stages of transforming union.[2] At those

1. *Writings,* p. 144.
2. See *Spiritual Journey,* pp. 41, 45-52, 97-226.

thresholds, our receptivity is permeated by an intensity and a quality which are truly of a superior order — "superior," that is, in comparison to our previous experiences.

In the concluding paragraphs of *The Mystical Milieu*,[3] Teilhard describes some superior qualities of that receptivity:

> Already at the earliest dawning of the mystical movement within the soul [i.e., our conscious quest for and communion with a personal loving God], the Lord is experienced as the only One who can sustain it and direct it.

Our ability and will to search relentlessly for a Power-greater-than-ourselves are received entirely from God. Moreover, they are sustained and directed by the Lord himself.

> The zest for life which is the source of all our passion and wisdom does not arise from ourselves . . . It is God alone who must give us even the impulse to seek him . . . We cannot do other than receive ourselves.

Yes, we undergo life as much as, if not more than, we undergo death. We receive not only our individual act of existence, but also our potentiality for becoming and our ability to actualize it.

> And even though the soul experiences itself on fire for heaven, it still cannot by itself see what it lacks in order to get there.

That statement captures the quintessence of passive purification: namely, even with the assistance of the most competent counseling and spiritual guidance, we come to know ourselves only so far. Beyond that point, God alone has the power to penetrate our inmost being so as to detach us from every trace of egocentrism. What do we do? We let that purification be done by him in his way and in his time.

3. See *Writings*, pp. 148-149.

Finally, when the soul has discerned the flaming Center that has been seeking it out, it remains powerless of itself to follow the divine Light all the way . . . The blessedness of transforming union is consummated in the realization of the absolutely gratuitous act of this supreme dependence on God.

Therefore, in terms of recovery from addiction, codependency and attachments, the Twelve-Step Program is but a first step. Beyond admitting that we are powerless over our addiction, we have to accept that we are also powerless before all our inner poverty. Beyond confessing that our life is unmanageable, we must give up trying to manage the utter gratuity of divine intimacy. Beyond believing that a Power-greater-than-ourselves can restore us to sanity, we have to acknowledge that the goal of recovery is not only sanity, but ultimately transformation in God by God. All those realizations catapult us into a receptivity of a superior order — that is, into an acquiescence transcendent to anything we had imagined at the outset of the recovery process.

In the essay *The Mystical Milieu,* Teilhard does not furnish examples of receptivity of a superior order. Throughout the course of his life, however, he does afford various concrete models. Among them, we select several which bear on the focus of this book, and we group them under five headings:

> the spiritual power of Matter;
> Teilhard's "third way";
> the phrase: "Everything that happens is adorable";
> the meaning of the cross;
> detachment by passing-all-the-way-through and by sublimation.

The first three examples pertain to the process of spiritualization inherent in the Twelve-Step Program. We present them in the remainder of this chapter. The last two examples address specifically the issue of pain, hurt and suffering which all recovering persons must undergo. We discuss them in the following chapter.

A. The Spiritual Power of Matter

> Matter is the ensemble of things, energies, creatures
> which surround us . . . It is the common, universal,
> tangible milieu infinitely varied and shifting within which
> we live. [4]

We experience Matter thus defined in basically two ways.

On the one hand, it is a burden. It fetters. Matter is the prime source of pain and sin which threaten our lives. It weighs us down. It wounds us and tempts us. It causes us to grow old. It makes us vulnerable. Matter in this sense is the context in which addiction, codependency and attachments occur. Who will deliver us from this body doomed to death (Rm 7:24)?

Yet, on the other hand and at the same time, Matter is what nourishes and uplifts us. It is physical exuberance, ennobling contact, sustained effort. It is the joy of growth and the matrix of development. Matter attracts, renews, unites, flowers. Who will give us this immortal body (1 Cor 15:42-53)?

(1) The Paradoxes of Matter

Matter is a fundamental principle of both death and life.

To illustrate the paradoxes of Matter, Teilhard uses the image of a mountain climber who, facing a slope enveloped in fog, struggles to climb to the summit bathed in light. That analogy offers two points of comparison regarding the relationship between Matter and human beings moving toward Spirit.

First, space is divided into two zones with opposing characteristics. The one behind grows ever darker as we advance. The zone up ahead becomes progressively luminous with each step forward.

Second, we are the ones who ascend or slip back. Matter only provides the support necessary for our movement.

---

4. *DM*, pp. 105-111 (and the same for all quotations unless otherwise identified in this section). See "The Spiritual Power of Matter" (1919) in *HM*, pp. 67-77; "The Names of Matter" (1919) in *HM* pp. 225-239.

In itself and prior to any position or choice on our part, Matter is simply the slope on which we can just as easily go up or down. We find ourselves situated at a specific point somewhere on the incline. In order to advance toward light, certain creatures are placed on our path as footholds to pass beyond and as intermediaries to use.

Upon the slope, true separation is made not exactly between Matter and Spirit, but rather between self-centering matter and spiritualizing matter. As a result of our initial position on the incline and as an outcome of each subsequent step, Matter is divided into that which is dominated by entropy and that which is giving way to evolution.

The great tragedy of addiction, codependency and attachment is that the person becomes riveted on matter in such a way as to set it in a self-centering direction. S/he gives in to entropy. On the other hand, to evolve matter in the direction of Spirit requires intense effort and much self-discipline; hence, a certain amount of suffering.

Spirit is that which Matter is becoming. Therefore, spiritualization is accomplished not by dematerializing oneself, but by letting Christ's Spirit spiritualize one's Matter.

(2) *Christ in Matter*

The analogy of the mountain climber describes the general ascent of Matter toward Spirit. In virtue of Christ's incarnation, death and resurrection, however, all evolution is being directed toward the Parousia. It is in Christogenesis. The movement is one — toward the highest possible degree of being. Its rhythm is twofold — immersion in creation for Christ and emergence through creation with Christ:[5]

> Matter, in you I find both seduction and strength, caresses and dynamism. You can enrich me or destroy me. I surrender myself to your mighty layers, trusting in the heavenly influences which have penetrated and purified

---

5. See *Spiritual Journey*, pp. 41, 45-50, 55-61, 99-113.

your deep waters. The power of Christ has passed into
you. May your allurement draw me forward. May your sap
nourish me. May your resistance make me strong. May
your detachments free me. And, finally, may your whole
being become the matrix of my divinization.

Abandonment of oneself to Matter with such indomitable
conviction and steadfast determination is awesome. In order
not to succumb to the temptation of matter, a person would
need a special grace, one emanating from a receptivity of a
superior order. Teilhard, for his part, expressed just such an
awareness in his *Journal* on 23 April 1919:

My life has to be a striking example of obedience . . . to
the universal operation of God. It must be an unflinching
act of faith in the "spiritual power of Matter."

Five years before his death, Teilhard leaves a mature
reflection concerning the seriousness of such a gift and
vocation:

Even at my age [sixty-nine], I am still learning by experience just how risky it is for one to be called to leave
behind the well-trodden path of a certain traditional
asceticism . . . Yet I have been forced by grace and by
inner necessity to search in the direction of heaven for a
way — one not mediocre, but superior — in which all the
dynamics of Matter and Flesh pass into the genesis of
Spirit . . . Yes, to Christify Matter! That sums up the
whole venture of my interior life. Although I am still often
frightened by its pursuit, I have never been able to do
other than take the required risk.[6]

B. *Teilhard's Third Way*

Just what is that way, not mediocre but superior, in which
all the dynamics of Matter and Flesh pass into the genesis of
Spirit?

6. "The Heart of Matter" (1950) in *HM*, pp. 46-47.

In a certain sense, Teilhard's *vía tértia* synthesizes his spirituality. It also sheds considerable light on the meaning he gives to the word "superior" in the phrase "receptivity of a superior order."

(1) *Matter Becoming Spirit*

In effect, the expression "third way" is a succinct formulation of an extremely complex and all-embracing reality. Teilhard often uses it in the sense of a *vía média*: that is, a way between two extremes, a way out of a dilemma, a way through an impasse. This middle or third way, however, is far from compromising, mediocre or neutral:

> It is a superior and daring way which recapitulates and corrects the values and characteristics of the other two ways [whatever they may be in a specific situation].[7]

The third way is like a synthesis in a dialectic, like a threshold in an evolution, like an emergence in a genesis.

In other words, the asceticism and mysticism of the *vía tertía* can take two opposing factions, digest out of each what is authentically of Spirit and then synthesize that into something superior to both. In Teilhard's personal life, the dilemma underlying this *vía média* was the dysfunctionality he experienced in an acute form of dualism: *either* love of Heaven *or* love of Earth; *either* cult of Spirit *or* cult of Matter. It took him almost half a lifetime to resolve the conflict for himself:

> We must go to Heaven through Earth. There exists true communion with God through the World. Moreover, to give oneself completely to that truth is not to contradict the Gospel and to try to serve two masters [Mt 6:24] . . . No, between the cult of Spirit which requires us to flee Matter and the cult of Matter which forces us to deny Spirit [there exists another possibility. It is detachment]

---

7. "The Atomism of Spirit" (1941) in *AE*, p. 56.

— detachment, however, no longer by running away from
Matter, but by passing-all-the-way-through it and by
sublimation of it. Spiritualization is not accomplished by
negation of or withdrawal from creatures but by [converg-
ence with them in Christ and by] emergence beyond them
in him.[8]

(2) *Flesh Becoming Spirit*

Perhaps nowhere are the asceticism and the mysticism of
the *vía tértia* applied in a more down-to-earth fashion than in
the question of celibate love. Also, in few places is the
tendency to become addicted, codependent or attached experienced with more proclivity than in the area of concupi-
scence and sexuality.

Teilhard underwent the agony and the ecstasy of the gift
not only of falling in love, but also of being in love with a
particular woman. Moreover, he perceived the ability to love
both deeply and celibately at the same time as the ultimate test
of his theology of attaining Spirit through Matter:

The living heart of the Tangible is the Flesh. And for
Man, Flesh is Woman . . . At the term of the spiritual
power of Matter, therefore, lies the spiritual power of the
Flesh and of the Feminine.[9]

Teilhard certainly does not intend the above assertions to
be taken in a chauvinistic manner. Nor are they pro-feminist,
anti-feminist or sexist in any way. On the contrary, he is trying
desperately to return to the pristine message of the Gospel and
to learn from the incarnation and resurrection of Christ how, in
the context of a celibate vocation, to grow in/through/with his
intense love for a specific person and his love for God. He

8. 'The Atomism of Spirit" (1941) in *AE*, pp. 53-57. See "Christology and Evolution" (1933)
   in *CE*, pp. 76-95
9. "The Heart of Matter" (1950) in *HM*, p. 58; "The Evolution of Chastity" (1934) in *TF*, p.
   70. See "The Eternal Feminine" (1918) in *Writings*, pp. 191-204.

experienced both loves as special graces to be lived not like parallel lines, but as divine gifts converging one upon the other in a deeper synthesis. Moreover, he was convinced that until he could integrate those passionate loves in interior harmony, peace and joy — despite the surface turbulence and tension that might persist — his convictions about the spiritual power of Matter would remain only a pipe dream:

> Theoretically, this transformation of love is possible. All that is needed to effect it is that the pull of the personal divine Center be experienced with sufficient force to transform our natural attraction . . .
>
> In practice, however, I must admit the difficulty of such an undertaking . . . Surely, you say, universal experience has proven conclusively that spiritual loves have always ended up in the mud. Well, you also said that humankind is meant to walk on the ground. Who could have ever dreamt that we would fly? [Much less walk on the moon!]
>
> Yes, I respond, some dreamers have dared . . . Yet, what paralyzes Life is the lack of faith and the refusal to risk. Life's greatest difficulty does not lie in solving problems, but in posing them correctly . . .
>
> Thus, the day will surely come — [indeed it is already here!] — when, after harnessing space, gravity, winds and tides, we shall harness for God the energies of love. And on that day, for the second time in the history of the World, humankind will have discovered fire. [10]

Needless to say, the grace to live day-in and day-out the formidable exigencies of this *vía tértia* does not pertain to some passivity of a compromising, mediocre or inferior way. It can arise only from a courageous receptivity of a superior order.

C. *Everything That Happens is Adorable*

Tout ce qui arrive est adorable. "Properly understood," Teilhard adds, "that saying summarizes the core of my reli-

---

10. "The Evolution of Chastity" (1934) in *TF*, pp. 86-87.

gious conviction."[11] It also explains in a practical way the continual and eventually final dominance of detachment in our mortal lives. Put another way, ultimate personal progress is achieved only in total surrender of self to a Power-greater-than-self.

Teilhard used a variation of that saying when he first spoke of the passivities of existence. "Oh, 'the joy of the action of the Other within us!' That is exactly what makes the passivities of existence appear so delicate to me and so worthy of adoration."[12] Moreover, Teilhard charges the French *adorable* with much more force than its English transliteration ordinarily conveys:

> To adore means to give of one's deepest to him whose depth has no end . . . to lose oneself unitively in God.[13]

Gradually, as he became more imbued with a receptivity of a superior order, Teilhard reflected more deeply on the significance of all passivities precisely as *adorables*. He explains that whatever befalls us, whether good or bad, eventually becomes adorable on the condition that we have done everything within our power to give Christic energy its full being and its full meaning in a concrete situation. In other words, something is truly adorable only when we have done our maximum to bestow on creatures the utmost reality that Christ desires us to give them and when we have left ourselves receptive to the optimum spiritual energy which they have to endow us.

Furthermore, the word *adorable* is not only an adjective. It also has the force of a proper name: *l'Adorable.* For "whatever we suffer, we undergo Christ." That is, we experience Christ himself while he suffers in us suffering. He and I endure

---

11. Letter to his brother Joseph, 13 Nov. 1943, in *LT*, pp. 288-289.
12. Letter to his cousin Marguerite, 28 Dec. 1916, in *MM*, p. 158.
13. *DM*, pp. 127-128: "The Evolution of Chastity" (1934) in *TF*, p. 65.
14. "Forma Christi" (1918), in *Writings*, p. 259; *Journal*, 28 Feb. 1919; "My Universe" (1918) in *HM*, p. 204; *DM*, p. 123.

pain and suffer each other together. We undergo each other for one another and on account of each other. *"Com-pátimur."*[14]

That attitude is the ultimate in Christian resignation. It is to commune with God in the deepest way possible this side of the resurrection. To experience *l'Adorable* in everything that happens is unquestionably a receptivity of a superior order. This is especially true when it is a question of the cross and of detachment, which we take up in the next chapter.

CHAPTER 17

RECEPTIVITY OF A SUPERIOR ORDER IN RELATION TO SUFFERING

The single most decisive influence driving people into addictions, codependency and attachments is avoidance of pain. Whether the pain is a specific trauma or a constellation of hurts, they experience it as intolerable. They are compelled to go to extremes to escape it. Innumerable factors contribute to the compulsion. High on the list of factors is the inability of addicted, codependent or attached persons to appreciate any positive or constructive meaning in the pain which imposes itself upon them. Quite literally, their suffering is a scandal, a "stumbling block" which they cannot surmount. It is an insanity, a "foolishness" which they cannot get over (1 Cor 1:23).

Clearly, no mortal wisdom, logic or rationale will ever satisfy our mind regarding human suffering. The cross is inherently insane from every experiential point of view. Yet there is another perspective: faith. In evangelical faith, human suffering can be experienced "as God's power to save" (1 Cor 1:18).

Undergoing the cross from a faith stance and accepting the painful wrenching inherent in detachment as integral to personal growth are essential to lasting recovery from addiction, codependency and attachments. With the insights of Pierre Teilhard de Chardin, we address those two issues in this chapter, namely: (1) the faith-imbued meaning of the cross in our daily lives, and (2) the positive thrust of detachment.

A. *The Meaning of the Cross*

The first two steps of the Twelve-Step Program for recovery stress the addict's admission of powerlessness over the fixation and belief in a Power-greater-than-self. A key to that admission and to that belief is this twofold experience: (1) the perception of one's powerlessness before the cross as something hope-filled, coupled with (2) the realization that what conventional wisdom and creaturely strength call foolishness and impotence in God is in reality inexhaustibly wiser than human wisdom and infinitely stronger than human power (1 Cor 1:25).

In the light of Christ, the cross can be experienced as "the symbol, the way and the act itself of making Progress."[1]

Teilhard calls the cross the symbol of Progress because it is the Christian sign par excellence of Jesus carrying the weight of the World in movement toward ultimate consummation. Jesus on the cross represents the blood, sweat and tears of all generations trying to make something better out of their lives and their surroundings — for themselves, for their progeny and for God.

The cross is also the way — indeed, the only true way — to spiritualization: "Our daily deaths, together with our personal death, are but so many thresholds sewn along the road to Union."[2]

The cross is, moreover, the very act of Progress by reason of this principle: The more perfect the union, the more intense the suffering. Or, as Teilhard expressed it in *The Phenomenon of Man* (1940, pp. 50-51):

> Every synthesis costs something . . . Nothing worthwhile is ever made except at the price of an equivalent destruction of energy . . . From an evolutionary standpoint, something is necessarily burnt up in the course of every synthesis in order to pay for it.

---

1. *DM*, pp. 101-104 (and the same for all quotations, unless otherwise identified, in this section).
2. "Sketch of a Personalistic Universe" (1936) in *HE*, p. 88.

Thus the cross is a sublime means which we must use in transcending ourselves. It is a necessary condition for attaining transformation.

The reality of the cross has always been a basic principle of selection and a sign of contradiction. It distinguishes the courageous from the pleasure-seekers, the serious from the frivolous, the sincere from the takers. Whether we prefer the word "cross," "night," "self-discipline," "asceticism" or some other term, the effect is the same: Each person who is convinced that true Progress lies up ahead at the cost of intense personal effort adheres by that very fact to the doctrine of the cross. Life has but one term, and it imposes only one direction: toward the highest possible spiritualization by means of maximum effort. Whoever puts forth his/her best effort to improve the World has already begun to follow the crucified Jesus. All conscientious human activity is necessarily an ascesis (cf. Rm 1:18-25; 8:18-25).[3]

Christianity offers certain specific insights to that basic truth. First, the mystery of the "sin of the world" (Jn 1:29) provides a deepened perception of the moral weaknesses inherent in the evolutionary process. Second, the unfathomable reality of the historical Jesus — especially in his mission and passion — testifies that authentic growth and goodness are "not to be sought in the temporal zones of our visible world, but that the effort required of our fidelity must be consummated beyond a total metamorphosis of ourselves and of everything around us."

The cross means "detachment from the sensate World, and even in a certain sense rupture with that World." At its core, the cross is a positive self-emptying which is born out of the wrenching thresholds of development. "It is the road of human effort divinely rectified and extended."

From a hedonistic standpoint, suffering and death — even effort and discipline — constitute the slagheap of nature and particularly of humanity. They are so much waste, refuse, rubbish to be disposed of, buried or incinerated. Yet to the

3. See "Cosmic Life" (1916) in *Writings*, pp. 65-68, 70-71.

person of prayer and faith, the cross recycles, so to speak, all
that debris in the direction of Spirit.

From a purely pragmatic stance, long-term and terminal
sufferers should be put out of their misery. They are useless
drains on society's resources. For whatever reason, they are
failures and must not be allowed to obstruct progress. The
mystery of the cross manifests not only the inhumanness of
such attitudes, but also the fact that they are absolutely un-
christian. For from the perspective of the Body of Christ, there
are many different organs and diverse functions. That charism
which is most charged with potential to advance the spiritual
Progress of the World is the *ádorans*, the contemplative. By
circumstance, sufferers are forced out of the realm of exterior
and material development into the realm of interior and
spiritual Progress — a veritable contemplative life. Thus, in a
most intense manner, sufferers carry the weight of the World in
Progress. By a mysterious act of providence, they have
paradoxically the capacity to become the most active con-
tributors to the same development that seems to have vic-
timized them.[4]

If the image of the cross is the way of spiritual transformation, then Jesus upon his cross is both the symbol and the
reality of the immense labor necessary to liberate Spirit. The
crucified Christ represents and recapitulates all the effort of
creation struggling together with God to ascend the slopes of
being:

> At times, we hold on to creatures to find support, at other
> times we are detached from them in order to go beyond
> them . . . The Cross, consequently, is not something
> inhuman, but something vastly suprahuman . . . For the
> Christian, it is not a question of swooning in its shadow,
> but of ascending in the light of the Cross.

Yes, the cross is definitely not something inhuman, but
suprahuman. The ability to accept it joyously — with open
arms, as it were — is truly a receptivity of a superior order.

4. See "The Significance and Positive Value of Suffering" (1933) in *HE*, pp. 48-52.

B. Detachment by Passing-All-The-Way-Through and by Sublimation

The twelfth step of the Twelve-Step Program for recovery speaks of a "spiritual awakening" which results from admitting one's powerlessness over the addiction and believing that only a Power-greater-than-self can restore one to sanity. That spiritual awakening launches the pilgrim well into his/her spiritual journey. In recovery from addictions and co-dependency, the sojourner is now equipped to face head-on the myriad of lingering attachments.

Those attachments are frequently difficult to identify and troublesome to eradicate because in so many instances they are subtly intermingled with qualities which need to be fostered. Moreover, many attachments remain the raw material for other potential addictions or the matrix for possible relapse into former dependencies.

Teilhard de Chardin affords penetrating insights into the process of detachment.

From an evolutionary point of view, detachment can no longer be understood primarily as rupture with the World, but rather as a passing-all-the-way-through creation and as a sublimation of it: *détachement par traversée et sublimation.*

(1) *Detachment from an Evolutionary Perspective*

In *The Phenomenon of Man* (1940, p. 218), Teilhard expresses his conviction regarding development as a whole:

> Is evolution a theory, a system or a hypothesis? It is much more. It is a general condition to which all theories, all systems, all hypotheses must bow and which they must henceforth satisfy if they are to be thinkable and true. Evolution is a light illuminating all facts; a curve that all lines must follow [including ascetical-mystical theology].

There exist innumerable theories concerning the particulars of the evolutionary process. Nonetheless, development as a general condition is an indisputable fact. Whether or not we advert to it, evolution has always been integral to the manner in which God effects transforming union. Evolution is God's way of creating and re-creating us.

Thus, long before Darwin or Teilhard, Christian mystics were swept along by a dynamic movement emanating from deep within the Gospel. That *élan* ascends relentlessly toward the Parousia. From the beginning, the person of Jesus has constituted its Alpha, its Way and its Omega (Rv 22:13; Jn 14:6). Yet the scientific evidence pointing to evolution as an all-embracing reality has shed enormous light on the mystery of life. Even though empirical evolution has been preoccupied almost exclusively with the outside of things (*le dehors*), it remains Teilhard's outstanding personal contribution to have uncovered scientifically the within of things (*le dedans*).

So how does evolution affect the high school dropout or the illiterate peasant? What does it mean to the humble mendicant of centuries past or to the otherwise sincere person of today who still is threatened by scientific evolution? Teilhard responds, first, one way:

> A person can be extremely "cosmic" in affection and tendency, while at the same time remaining rigorously detached in the narrowest and most austere sense of the term. That is, a Trappist can live a truly open interior life, even if he still thinks that the world is flat and that he must be cut off from all its machinations . . . Stark detachment, such as practiced by the great contemplative orders, should not be viewed in contrast to or in rupture with the arduous labor of cosmic Evolution. On the contrary, their asceticism is a flourishing and a prolongation of Evolution, [even if they do not directly advert to that fact].[5]

And then another:

5. *Journal,* 20 Oct. and 5 Nov. 1916.

> It would not only be useless, but also wrong to try to find in the Saints of the past explicit approval or condemnation of what I call cosmic asceticism, since the question of Evolution proper never entered their minds. What is necessary, however, is that, when we translate their quest for holiness into today's terms, we are able to see that indeed their detachment was by being-attached-to-Someone-greater-than-themselves (*détachement par sur-attachement*) . . . [In other words, their ascesis of spiritualization was not in effect] anti-Matter or extra-Matter, but trans-Matter.[6]

Trans-Matter: that is, (a) Christ transforming Matter in Spirit, and (b) God divinizing us through our Matter.

(2) *Detachment No Longer Understood Primarily as a Rupture with the World*

By reason of the element of discontinuity inherent in the evolutionary process, there is literally a leaving behind, a separation, a form of rupture in every detachment. This is most evident in the case of death. Furthermore, all that pertains to the machinations, the self-centeredness, the self-indulgent aspects of the world (Jn 1:10-11) must be cut off and left behind (Jn 15:1-5; Mt 13:42, 50).

Regarding detachment, however, Teilhard insists that the negative element is not primary. Severance and sometimes even fracture are the results of a fundamentally positive thrust. It is because conversion is toward God that we turn away from sin. It is because our commitment is to Christ that we give up whatever is holding us back from further christification.

During Teilhard's time the phrase *Da nóbis, Dómine, terréna despícere* — Grant us, O Lord, [the desire] to despise everything terrestrial — occurred frequently in the prayers of the Mass and the Breviary. Needless to say, that expression irritated Teilhard no end. Nevertheless, he did try to give it as favorable an interpretation as possible:

---

6. "A Note on the Concept of Christian Perfection" (1942), in *TF*, pp. 105-106.

Fortunately, that sentiment can be reconciled with "cosmic love" provided we understand *despícere* in the sense of "to regard as secondary" and *terréna* as "things loved for themselves without reference to Christ." Nonetheless, it seems that there has been a significant evolution in Christian consciousness on this subject. Sanctification is envisaged less as a work of rupture with or withdrawal from creation than as a love of detached involvement [*un amour du travail désintéressé*].[7]

What is that detached involvement — or, as he put it in *The Divine Milieu* (1927, p. 120): a passionate equanimity regarding all things (*une indifférence passionnée*)? It means . . .

(3) *Detachment by Passing-All-the-Way-Through Creation and by Sublimation*

Teilhard has his own way of expressing the dialectic between what John of the Cross called *todo* (all) and *nada* (nothing):

> Everything is both All to me and nothing.
> Everything is both God to me and dust.[8]

Every creature is from God, to God and with the proper nuances capable of being transformed in God. Yet the creature is not the Lord, nor will it become God in himself. That truth constitutes the gist of what Teilhard terms cosmic life, cosmic love, cosmic ascesis, cosmic mysticism. The ability to live that reality peacefully and joyfully is at the core of being a fully integrated Christian.

Teilhard's theology of suffering and detachment sheds considerable light on maintaining a passionate equanimity regarding all things. Most eighteenth- and nineteenth-century interpretations of pain can be summarized thus:

7. *Journal*, 10 May 1916. See *Cor.*, pp. 72-74.
8. *DM*, p. 120. See *DM*, pp. 95-101; *Writings*, pp. 70-71, 259-264.

Suffering is first and foremost a punishment, an expiation.

Its effectiveness derives from the fact that it hurts. In fact, the more it hurts the more efficacious it is.

Suffering is born of sin and makes up for sin. That is why sacrifice, penance and reparation are needed.

Thus, it is good to suffer, to deny oneself, to inflict pain and deprivation upon oneself.

In contrast to that view which we would term Jansenistic, an evolutionary perspective casts the same mystery in a vastly different light:

Suffering and detachment are primarily the consequence of the labor of development and the price that has to be paid for Progress.

Their effectiveness derives from the love and the generosity of persons whose blood, sweat and tears contribute to making a better World for Christ.

Pain and sin are the by-products of the process of becoming, for everything that develops suffers and commits its own faults.

The Cross is the symbol of the arduous task of Evolution.

Thus, by the Cross the sin of the World is taken away.

Suffering and detachment pertain then to evangelical poverty, Christian asceticism, *détachement par traversée*.

Detachment by going-all-the-way-through denotes this: In full discipleship with the Incarnate Word, we become deeply involved not only with creation as the sum total of creatures, but also with creation as the ongoing process of Evolution. God creates by means of development towards an ultimate point of consummation. Thus, we become involved in creation in such a way as to go-all-the-way-through it to its term which is recapitulation of all in Christ (Col 1:20). If we follow the Lord unreservedly in his involvement, then we must also eventually die with him to all so as to rise with him beyond all.

At this point, Teilhard adds a further insight: namely, detachment is not only a question of passing-all-the-way-through but also of sublimation. For some people, that word in English conjures up repression. For Teilhard, however, "sublimation" draws attention to what is retained transcendently in and after detachment.

In detached involvement, we experience not only discontinuity with respect to creatures but also continuity. Passing through creation, we bring along with us in a purified and transformed manner the qualitative quintessence of everything in our World. In this sense, detachment is not exactly the opposite of attachment. It is rather a rectified and spiritualized *surattachement* — an attachment-to-Someone-beyond-ourselves. It is "a kind of transformed attachment like spirit is transformed matter and internationalism is transformed patriotism."[9] In this way, we involve ourselves in creation with passionate equanimity. We experience that we have need of everything and that we have need of nothing; that the One-Thing-Necessary (Lk 10:41) comprises everything.

On the occasion of his interior crisis during the battle of Verdun, Teilhard expresses in his *Journal* (17 July 1916) a personal integration of the various aspects of detachment:

> We must go to God with our whole heart [Mt 22:37]. That means not only with our heart as a capacity for loving, but especially our heart as actually filled with concrete loves . . . Our conversion to God does not consist in emptying our heart and then substituting him for all our loves. No, our conversion consists rather in assimilating in him all our loves in their concrete fullness.

Thus we allow the Lord to purify our loves and to transform them. We encounter God in those we love to the degree that both we and they become progressively spiritualized.

9. *Journal*, 9 May 1921.

Christ is not a substitution for our loves. Rather, they are sublimated in him. That is, we gradually experience them according to his manner of involvement and detachment — in his *kenosis* (Ph 2:7).

Involvement and detachment — like breathing in and breathing out. That is the true breath of the mystic, the searcher, the pilgrim, the person recovering from addiction, codependency or attachment of any sort. Through involvement and detachment, we let a Power-greater-than-ourselves restore us to sanity by integrating our life.

Could anyone seriously doubt that the lived experience of detachment as being-attached-to-Someone-beyond-oneself in all its day-in and day-out implications pertains to a receptivity of a superior order? Moreover, it is a receptive stance to which we are all invited, since each person — no matter how addicted, codependent or attached — is called to transforming union.

CONCLUSION

This book has been a study of theological underpinnings for recovery from addiction, codependency and attachment according to St. John of the Cross and Pierre Teilhard de Chardin.

Numerous factors differentiate John and Teilhard: historical and cultural milieus, individual vocations and personalities, world views and interior experiences. Each expresses his convictions regarding detachment out of an intimate experience of God within him and all around him. While remaining remarkably unique and personal in their respective perceptions and presentations, both converge on the Gospel as lived in the pristine ascetical and mystical tradition of Judeo-Christianity.

We might summarize the quintessence of John of the Cross's theology as it relates to detachment this way: Although he possesses a balanced teaching on the immanence of God, John consistently accentuates the divine transcendence and the *nada* of everything created. God's immanence is itself transcendent. John explicitly recognizes the necessity of our involvement in creation and our consequent passing-all-the-way-through, but he stresses what lies beyond the passage. To encounter God in himself infinitely transcends attaining his presence through or within creation. The quest for a Power-greater-than-ourselves through creatures must lead ultimately to immediate communion with the Lord beyond them all. The Christ of John of the Cross is the Jesus of St. Paul and of the Gospel, but John accentuates his kenosis. John's asceticism is founded almost entirely on *desnudez*. Its thrust is positive and dynamic, at the same time straight and narrow. He is the co-reformer of Carmel, the apostle of direct and loving transformation in the Beloved in contemplation.

The quintessence of Teilhard's theology as it relates to detachment can be summarized thus: Although the transcendence of God remains the beginning and the end of his immanence, Teilhard stresses his Diaphany: God all in all (1 Cor 15:28; Ep 1:23), God through all (Rm 1:20; 8:22). The Christ of Teilhard is the personal Jesus of St. Paul and of the Gospel, but he accentuates the Cosmic Christ, the Universal Christ, Christ the Evolver. Teilhard's asceticism is also cosmic. It is situated in a renewed World vision. Its transversal movement (i.e., its going-all-the-way-through) is constituted by an immersion into the World for Christ, followed by an emergence through the World with him, with a continual and eventually final dominance of the second over the first. That élan comprises both the vertical and the horizontal in such a way that the On-High and the Up-ahead converge toward the Christic. Detachment is accomplished by going-all-the-way-through and by being-attached-to-Someone-beyond-oneself. Spiritualization is effected not by becoming anti-Matter or extra-Matter, but by being drawn trans-Matter; that is, by letting God cause Matter to become Spirit. Teilhard is the apostle of communion with God through the Earth.

Addictions, codependency and attachments are fundamentally spiritual problems. Many facets enter into a holistic appreciation of the human person: familial and private; social and individual; ecclesial and civil; physical, emotional, mental and spiritual. All those factors interact and complement one another. They contribute to an integrated life. Yet the more a person matures, the more those diverse aspects converge upon and are ultimately synthesized in one — the spiritual.[1]

The relationship of addiction, codependency and attachment to the spiritual life is not new to Judeo-Christianity. Both

---

1. See *Spiritual Journey*, pp. 19-32; *Spiritual Direction*, pp. 25-31.

Testaments are replete with imagery stressing movement from isolation to communion, from selfishness to conversion, from sin to salvation, from slavery to redemption.

In the Hebrew Scriptures, for example, the Power-greater-than-ourselves is frequently presented as

> *Yahweh Sabaoth* — the Lord of Armies —
> who delivers us from our enemies.

Let no one doubt that our most formidable oppressors are the hosts of inner fixations which hold us captive and the warring compulsions which have the potential to drive us insane.

In the New Testament, for instance, the Power-greater-than-ourselves is revealed as

> *Abba* — Father, Dad —
> whose steadfast fidelity impels him to wait as long as it
> takes for our return (Lk 15:20-24);
> who goes out to meet us even as we refuse to come in
> (Lk 15:25-32);
> whose everlasting tenderness forces him to leave the
> ninety-nine in search of the lost one (Lk 15:3-7);
> who works with us in everything so that we are not
> definitively separated from his love made visible in
> Christ Jesus our Lord (Rm 8:15, 28-39).

Psychology, John of the Cross and Teilhard de Chardin present basically the same truths about recovery from addiction, codependency and attachment. Yet each of the three perspectives uses its own terminology and contains its own insights regarding the starting point of the problem, together with the means and the goal of the recovery process:

Psychology. Here the starting point is a lack of self-love resulting in most instances from an experience of insufferable pain. The means for recovery is admission that one's life is out of control, coupled with the gradual restoration of one's will to live in the real world with the help of a Power-greater-than-oneself. The goal of the process is peace, happiness and connectedness with self and significant others.

John of the Cross. His starting point is inner poverty, or that host of immaturities within us which cause us to fix our will upon some person, situation or thing. The crux of recovery is the dark night of the soul which stitch-by-stitch strips and detaches us of all that is not God in himself. The goal of the process is radical transformation of ourselves and of all our loves in God, by God.

Teilhard de Chardin. His starting point for addiction, codependency and attachment is our succumbing to inert passivities, or the temptation of matter which is rooted in the self-centering energies of entropy, or the sin of the world. The key to recovery lies in our gradual recognition and subsequent surrender to the passivities of existence, of growth, or diminishment and ultimately to a receptivity of a superior order. The goal of the process is zest for the Real, spiritualization of Matter, divinization of all that we do and undergo, recapitulation of all in Christ.

Be it the Twelve-Step Program, *desnudez,* or cosmic ascesis, the hurt we fall victim to, the misery we cause ourselves and others, the pain we undergo from both within and without — in other words, all our human suffering — can become the matrix not only of recovery and new life, but also of an entirely new creation and of transformation in God.

Sic finis volúminis,
non aútem itíneris.

SELECT BIBLIOGRAPHY

We gratefully acknowledge the following works which were our primary sources for the psychological perspective on addiction and codependency presented in the first section of this book.

Beattie, Melody. *Codependent No More*. San Francisco: Harper & Row, 1987.

_____. *Beyond Codependency*. San Francisco: Harper & Row, 1989.

Bradshaw, John. *Bradshaw On: Healing the Shame That Binds You*. Deerfield Beach: Health Communications, 1988.

Carnes, Patrick. *Out of the Shadows: Understanding Sexual Addiction*. Minneapolis: CompCare Publishers, 1983.

Firestone, Robert. *The Fantasy Bond: Effects of Psychological Defenses on Interpersonal Relations*. New York: Human Sciences Press, 1985.

Fossum, Merle A. and Mason, Marilyn J. *Facing Shame: Families in Recovery*. New York: Norton, 1986.

Kaufman, Gershen. *Shame: The Power of Caring*. Rochester: Shenkman Books, 1980.

Miller, Alice. *For Your Own Good: Hidden Cruelty in Child-rearing and the Roots of Violence*. New York: Farrar, Straus, Giroux, 1983.

_____. *The Drama of the Gifted Child: The Search for the True Self*. New York: Basic Books, 1981.

Nakken, Craig. *The Addictive Personality: Roots, Rituals, Recovery.* Center City: Hazelden, 1988.

Napier, Augustus with Whitaker, Carl. *The Family Crucible: The Intense Experience of Family Therapy.* New York: Harper and Row, 1978.

Schaeffer, Brenda. *Is It Love or Is It Addiction? Falling into Healthy Love.* New York: Harper & Row, 1987.

Washton, Arnold and Boundy, Donna. *Willpower's Not Enough: Understanding and Recovering from Addictions of Every Kind.* New York: Harper & Row, 1989.

Weihold, Barry and Weihold, Janae. *Breaking Free of the Codependency Trap.* Walpole: Stillpoint Publishing, 1989.